D1200853

Conceptual Foundations
of Business Research

Conceptual Foundations of Business Research

PAUL H. RIGBY

Professor of Business Administration
Director, Bureau of Business Research
The Pennsylvania State University

John Wiley and Sons, Inc.,   New York   London   Sydney

330.72
R56c

Copyright © 1965 by John Wiley & Sons, Inc.
All rights reserved. This book or any part thereof
must not be reproduced in any form without the
written permission of the publisher.

Library of Congress Catalog Card Number: 65-12701
Printed in the United States of America

SECOND PRINTING, FEBRUARY, 1966

To my grandmother, Ella Rigby

MAR 9 - '67

THE HUNT LIBRARY
CARNEGIE INSTITUTE OF TECHNOLOGY

Preface

Scientific business research does considerably more than collect data and report facts. It develops new concepts and principles, tests hypotheses, builds models, and contributes to theory. It studies techniques for problem solving and decision making. And it develops new or improved solutions to operational problems of the business firm.

This is a concept of business research which is relatively new and is much broader than that traditionally used. Typically, business research has been limited to fact gathering—to the collection, as accurately as possible, of those data needed to describe or report on events, practices, or conditions such as customers' buying habits, managerial practices, community purchasing power, or manufacturers' sales' trends. Often insufficient thought has been given to the development and testing of concepts, hypotheses, principles, and theories or to their use in problem solving and decision making. Occasionally some of these terms are used but not always correctly.

Because of their narrow orientation, traditional business researchers have had a limited understanding of the contribution that business research can make to a discipline and to decision making in the business firm. They have not distinguished among reporting, description, and explanation. They have not fully appreciated the contribution that the abstract knowledge of a basic discipline can contribute to the firm's efforts to solve problems and make decisions—for example, the possible relationships between microeconomic theory and a study to develop a monthly report evaluating a public relations department.

The problem is not the failure of business researchers to learn the techniques and tools for conducting research, because they do acquire them. In the course of their education, most learn statistical techniques; some become skilled in writing questionnaires; many familiarize themselves in detail with sources of information; others become proficient in mathematical analysis and programming computers. Although business researchers may need to learn even more about techniques, their notable weakness is their inadequate emphasis on the research process. Knowing how to use the tools and techniques of research does not in itself guarantee the effectiveness of an individual in carrying out a scientific investigation.

This neglect of the research process is due to the restricted contact which business researchers have had with the epistemology of science. Undoubtedly, both the newness of business administration as a formal discipline and of its research efforts helps to explain this current fledgling state of scientific business research. Another and possibly more important explanation is the failure of business schools to develop programs conducive to research and an understanding of research. A number of observers have emphasized this failure. Among the most notable examples are statements in the two reports, *Higher Education for Business* by Gordon and Howell and *The Education of the American Businessman* [1] by Pierson and others. Both are critical of the type and quality of business research being conducted in business schools. Gordon and Howell make the following statement:

> Much if not most research in business schools attempts merely to describe current practice or, going a short step further, to develop normative rules which summarize what is considered to be the best of prevailing practice. The business literature is not, in general, characterized by challenging hypotheses, well developed conceptual frameworks, the use of sophisticated research techniques, penetrating analysis, the use of evidence drawn from relevant underlying disciplines—or very significant conclusions. [2]

If what Gordon and Howell say is correct, the existing level of research in business schools would certainly help to explain

[1] Robert A. Gordon and James Edwin Howell, *Higher Education for Business*, Columbia University Press, New York, 1959. Frank C. Pierson and others, *The Education of American Businessmen*, McGraw-Hill Book Co., New York, 1960.
[2] Gordon and Howell, *op. cit.*, p. 379.

the limited understanding that a number of business researchers have of research.

The business researcher needs to learn that there is a distinction between research tools and techniques and the research process. He should have an insight into the formation of concepts and the significance of new concepts to thinking about a given phenomena. He should understand the relationship among empirical observations, generalizations, principles, laws, and theories. If, in addition, he also knows techniques which are pertinent to his field of study, he will be in a reasonably good position to understand and conduct research.

Russell L. Ackoff in his book *Scientific Method: Optimizing Applied Research Decisions,* seeks to distinguish among tools, techniques, and methods.

By a scientific *tool* we mean a physical or conceptual *instrument* that is used in scientific inquiry. Examples of such tools are mathematical symbols, electronic computers, microscopes, tables of logarithms and random numbers, thermometers, and cyclotrons.[3]

By a scientific "technique" Ackoff has in mind "a way of accomplishing a scientific objective, a scientific *course of action.* Techniques, therefore, are ways of using scientific tools." [4] The term "method" he uses to refer to the procedure followed in selecting the technique to be used in a specific situation.

These three terms and their implications deal with one area with which a researcher should become acquainted; and as stated previously, the one aspect with which business students do become acquainted, particularly with tools and techniques. However, defining "method" somewhat more broadly than Ackoff does would describe the other aspects of research—understanding the basic strategy and approach of scientific investigation. The following statement by Paul F. Lazarsfeld and Morris Rosenberg in the introduction of the book, *The Language of Social Research,* suggests these other pertinent parts of *"method."* In their discussion of methodology they say:

[3] Russell L. Ackoff with the collaboration of Shiv K. Gupta and J. Sayer Minas, *Scientific Method: Optimizing Applied Research Decisions,* John Wiley and Sons, New York, 1962, p. 5.
[4] *Ibid.,* p. 5.

The term methodology seems more appropriate. It implies that concrete studies are being scrutinized as to the procedures they use, the underlying assumptions they make, the modes of explanation they consider as satisfactory. Methodological analysis in this sense provides the elements from which a future philosophy of the social sciences may be built. If our linguistic feeling is adequate, the term should convey a sense of tentativeness; the methodologist codifies on going research practices to bring out what is consistent about them and deserves to be taken into account the next time. Methodology and the related activities of explication and critical analysis have developed as a bent of mind rather than as a system of organized principles and procedures.[5]

If we interpret the term "method" broadly, it could be used to describe the topic of this book, which has been designed to discuss the conceptual problems of business research. I have assumed that these basic conceptual problems are common to all fields of business administration. Although tools and techniques for conducting research are not the subject here, it is my hope that the book can serve in a complementary capacity to books which do discuss them.

This book seeks to provide the reader with an understanding of the kind of problems which scientific research seeks to solve and the approach it takes in solving them. It indicates the information which research seeks to develop and its various contributions to problem solving and decision making in the business firm. The book considers the significance of research findings in the social sciences for business research. Specific techniques for conducting research are discussed only as they may provide examples to illustrate the conceptual problems being discussed. There are two good reasons for this. The first, of course, is the fact that techniques are not the subject of this book. The underlying assumption in my preparation was that research itself is a topic apart from techniques and tools. Second, so much material has been published dealing with techniques that it would be virtually impossible to attempt to cover in one book the many techniques that are of significance to business research. Many techniques can themselves justifiably fill a book. Furthermore, the techniques of significance to one field of business can be quite different from those of interest to another.

[5] Paul F. Lazarsfeld and Morris Rosenberg, Editors, *The Language of Social Research,* The Free Press of Glencoe, Illinois, 1955, p. 4.

The book has been based on eleven years of experience in personal research, the administration of programs to aid and support faculty research and teaching research seminars for graduate students in business administration. In general, the book follows the sequence of topics covered in the seminars. Since the seminars were for graduate students in all fields of business administration, the emphasis was on conceptual problems of research rather than the techniques or the specific theory of any field or discipline. The techniques and the theory of the various fields in business administration tend to vary greatly and so the seminars concentrated on basic conceptual problems of business research. This approach in the seminars has proved to be an effective one.

The book emphasizes the basic building blocks of scientific research. It discusses the formation and the role of concepts and the development of generalizations, principles, and theories. This material is designed to provide the reader with an insight into the epistemology of scientific study. Only too frequently the scientific method is either defined as the use of the experiment by physical scientists or simply the "objective collection of facts."

To broaden the reader's perspective of the potential contribution of business research, the book analyzes a variety of purposes and objectives in scientific business research, the role it can play in solving operational problems of the business firm and in the development of systematic knowledge in the fields of business administration. Applied research is analyzed in terms of the problem-solving and decision-making process. The growing role of the social sciences in problem-solving research in business is reviewed, emphasizing the relationship between theory and applied research.

In both basic and applied business research there has been inadequate use of the research design. A chapter has, therefore, been included which discusses research planning, emphasizing the nature of planning rather than a step by step formula.

Lastly there is a review of the problems of concept formation and definition, model construction, development of measures, and the collection of data and their relationship to scientific investigation.

The book should prove useful in any course dealing with business research. It should serve very well to supplement a book on techniques. The book should also prove helpful to professional business researchers and to people who find themselves administering, using, and evaluating business research.

A number of people were very helpful in the preparation of this book through their criticisms and suggestions. I would especially like to acknowledge I. E. McNeill, David M. Robinson, and W. T. Tucker who read and evaluated early drafts of this manuscript. Their comments were most helpful. I also wish to express my appreciation to Rondal G. Downing, whose excellent logic and understanding of scientific research assisted me in clarifying a number of ideas. Lastly, I am very grateful to Mrs. Harold Miederhoff for both her skill and cheerfulness in typing the manuscript and assisting in those many other chores associated with the preparation of a manuscript.

PAUL H. RIGBY

University Park, Pennsylvania
October, 1964

Contents

1

Modern Business Research

Business administration, like engineering and medicine, is an applied art rather than a science. It is concerned primarily with using knowledge to solve problems rather than with increasing knowledge. But like engineering and medicine, business administration should be scientific in solving problems. It should be acquainted with the knowledge which has been developed in related scientific fields of study, particularly mathematics, statistics, and the social sciences—political science, sociology, anthropology, and economics—and should proceed in a scientific manner to apply this knowledge. When it becomes necessary or desirable for business administration itself to contribute to knowledge, it should proceed as though it were a science.

SCIENCE IN ENGINEERING AND MEDICINE

Engineering and medicine have a long tradition of emphasizing scientific knowledge [1] and method in problem solving. Engineering relies heavily on the related fields of science, such as mathematics, physics, chemistry, and geology; and when developing knowledge, it proceeds as though it were a science. Similarly, medicine relies on such fields as chemistry, pathology, physiology, anatomy, bacteriology, and statistics. When conducting its own

---

[1] Scientific knowledge is defined here as a systematic body of concepts, theories, principles, and laws or law-like statements designed to explain phenomena.

research, it adheres quite rigidly to the scientific method. The medical profession, in fact, is particularly well-known for its emphasis on classic scientific procedures. Sometimes the profession is even criticized when its emphasis on scientific procedures is interpreted as overcautiousness or undue conservatism.

Though engineers and physicians are not normally considered scientists (in the abstract sense), they are both expected to have sound scientific training. It is unthinkable for either group to receive a professional education without preparation in their related sciences. Their respective professional associations have instituted various measures which insure this, through either the associations that accredit their schools, requirements for public certification to practice, or both.

SCIENCE IN BUSINESS ADMINISTRATION

The idea of stressing science in business administration is still relatively new, even in colleges and universities. In fact, it represents a significant development which is currently taking place in the evolution of business administration. The trend can be found in the better schools of business and in the larger corporations. It is illustrated by the work of people in management science and operations research.

Apparently, this phase in the evolution of business administration is quite similar to one which has been experienced by other applied fields as they matured. W. Allen Wallis, formerly Dean of the University of Chicago Graduate School of Business, offers medicine as a typical example:

In the history of medical education, of legal education, of engineering education, or of education for any profession, there appears a strikingly similar pattern: an evolution from the teaching of current practice toward the teaching of underlying sciences; and evolution from the organization of materials around common practical situations to their organization around common intellectual content.

For instance, in medical education throughout all of western Europe except the Germanic countries, teaching in the nineteenth century was done by practitioners in hospitals through a system of apprenticeship. Education consisted of the observation of the practice of medicine, together with discussion of that practice. This system was admirably adapted to preventing new kinds of error, but it did not promote the discovery of new truths or a profound and growing understanding of health, disease, and therapy.

In the Germanic countries, on the other hand, medical education took place in universities through professors, and a thorough training in the preclinical sciences of physiology, anatomy, biochemistry, and pathology preceded introduction of the students into the clinics. An understanding of the preclinical sciences gave the students that broad general understanding of disease and therapy that would enable them to cope with new problems and discoveries. By the twentieth century, it was generally recognized that the Germanic system was far more effective in producing competent practitioners, and that system is followed today in all of the leading medical schools of Europe and America.[2]

Until rather recently schools of business administration, like the medical schools in the early nineteenth century, have adhered closely to the policy of teaching current practices—paying little attention to the scientific approach in problem solving, the application of knowledge from related fields of science, or the scientific practices in developing knowledge. Although the programs of most schools of business administration are still heavily influenced by this policy, it is slowly being replaced by one which emphasizes the scientific approach. This new policy insists that people in business administration—and particularly those receiving a university education, as is the case with engineers and physicians—should be thoroughly prepared in related fields of science and in the scientific approach to problem solving; that they should understand these related fields of science so well that they will be fully aware of their potential contribution to the solution of business problems; and that they should so thoroughly understand the scientific method that they will always be conscious of it when solving problems, and when necessary, searching for new knowledge.

The steps that are being taken to increase the role of science and scientific knowledge in business administration should not be confused with steps which are being taken to insure a liberal education for business students. Engineers do not study physics

---

[2] W. Allen Wallis, The Business of Schools of Business, *Business Horizons*, II (Spring, 1959) p. 103.

to liberalize their education but rather to understand a field critical to engineering. For this reason, business students should study psychology because it is a field critical to business.

TRADITIONAL BUSINESS RESEARCH

The impact of this reorientation is probably no greater anywhere than it is on business research. It has, for all practical purposes, introduced a new concept of business research which is radically different from the traditional one. Traditional business research has been limited to little more than fact gathering and reporting, using familiar data-gathering techniques such as the survey, interview, questionnaire, and sample. Typical studies would include reporting on consumer attitudes, collecting industrial statistics, and describing business practices. The statistical techniques of traditional business research—the frequency distribution, measures of central tendency, and the trend line—are fundamentally descriptive. Analysis of traditional research has too often been vague and superficial, doing little more than suggesting the meaning or significance of the data reported. Because of its narrow orientation, traditional business research has contributed little toward improving problem solving and decision making or to understanding business. These contributions have come from other disciplines such as psychology, a field whose members are steeped in scientific methods and atuned to the importance of scientific knowledge.

The results of overemphasis on fact gathering by traditional business research can be seen in the typical community surveys. Throughout the United States a variety of organizations have conducted community surveys in which data are collected and classified on various aspects of the community: climate, geology, soils, agriculture, water, population, labor force, community services, manufacturing, retailing, and so on. These reports are valuable in the way that a statistical abstract is valuable. They provide valuable facts on community life, and to someone who understands the community they can be meaningful. But the weakness of community surveys as research efforts is their failure to present any kind of explanation to help anyone understand the community. The interpretation that usually accompanies a typical survey is superficial, vague, and general and without a sound theoretical basis. The techniques of analysis are elementary. The community surveys are similar to a census that might be taken of a community. A census provides a wide variety of valuable data, but its significance is revealed through analysis based on theory and hypothesis. The failure to properly analyze the data collected explains why so many surveys commence gathering dust almost the moment they are completed. Illustrative of efforts to make community studies more scientific is the use of input-output analysis which seeks to study regularities and patterns prevailing in a community's consumption and production. There is no doubt that the usual community surveys can be very helpful and valuable; however, they should not be considered research efforts but data collection.

We can better appreciate the limitations of traditional business research when we consider it in relation to the full range of scientific research activities. Roy G. Francis in *The Rhetoric of Science*,[3] suggests that scientific investigation falls into three categories. "Inquiry" or "qualitative research" is the work of the scientist who speculates, asks questions, and formulates hypotheses to explain phenomena. The process of rigorously testing ideas developed during the stage of "inquiry" through the use of techniques such as the experiment and statistical analysis he designates as "research" or "quantitative research." The third category he labels "analysis." Francis says of this phase:

When theoretical relations are not doubted, but only the world of fact, we have analysis. Appealing to a technique of information-gathering (as in a survey or census), analysis accepts theory as being true in order to permit an interpretation of the data. Thus one may survey a city to determine the status of housing. Then, believing a theory that relates housing to delinquency, one can interpret the data to point out danger spots, and so on.

Clearly, analysis is geared to practical activity; first, because no doubt is permitted, and hence no test is included or possible; second, because it is fastened to a unique historical situation. The survey is concerned with the here and now. The data are analyzed for immediate use.[4]

---

[3] Roy G. Francis, *The Rhetoric of Science,* University of Minnesota Press, Minneapolis, Minn., 1961.
[4] *Ibid.,* pp. 160–161.

Traditional business research has tended to ignore all three of these activities with the possible exception of "analysis," which some might prefer to label "interpretation." Since business administration is not a basic discipline such as economics or sociology but an applied field, it can be argued that an emphasis on interpretation is certainly appropriate; however, very little business research can be classified even under what Francis considers to be "analysis." Most of it can more appropriately be thought of as fact gathering or reporting. Where its research can be considered to be "analysis," it has typically been superficial and based on inadequate or poorly conceived theory.

One of the three categories which Robert Brown uses for classifying scientific investigation in the social sciences comes a little closer to describing the work of traditional business research. Brown draws a distinction between reporting, description, and explanation. In his book, *Explanation in Social Science*,[5] he considers "reporting" as including that research which restricts itself to giving an accurate account of an event or series of events but does not seek to give an explanation for the events. He considers "description" as including those efforts which seek not only to give an account of what took place but also to explain and give an understanding of specific events. Those efforts which attempt to generalize from empirical observations he would consider "explanation." The work of business research has, for the most part, been limited to what Brown would call reporting. It has some descriptions but virtually no explanations. If we were to borrow from Francis and Brown we could say that business research has been limited almost exclusively to reporting and analysis (or "interpretation").

Still another framework for regarding research is to classify it as either basic or applied research. Basic research is concerned with the development of knowledge to explain phenomena, while applied research is the development of new or improved solutions to operational problems. Traditional business research has tended to ignore both. Much of the basic research in the field

---

[5] Robert Brown, *Explanation in Social Science*, Aldine Publishing Co., Chicago, 1963.

of business administration has been done by economists, sociologists, and cultural anthropologists. Applied research, where it has been conducted as a conscientious effort, has usually been done ignoring the findings of basic research and the knowledge of the basic disciplines. The efforts have been devoted instead to reporting such information as business practices and procedures, customer attitudes, and industry statistics. This pattern, however, as Dean Wallis indicated is typical of the early period of a profession's development—illustrated by the early work in medical schools. The effort has been to emphasize reporting accepted practices and procedures rather than searching for new knowledge and new problem-solving techniques.

FACT GATHERING—IMPORTANT BUT NOT RESEARCH

Without any doubt, the work of fact gathering and classification is important and makes a valuable contribution to knowledge. In fact, this type of activity can represent the beginning of a scientific effort to develop knowledge in a field. This work of traditional business research can be compared to the work of the naturalist who has indeed made valuable contributions to basic knowledge through his work of collecting and classifying data on wild life. Similarly, the work of the United States Census has provided us with invaluable information not only on the nation's economy but also on almost every aspect of our society. The reporting of business practices or industry statistics has provided valuable information. Consumer surveys give significant clues to consumer behavior and their value should not be underestimated.

But data collection and classification alone, no matter how carefully or how accurately done, are only a part of scientific research. In addition to gathering facts, scientific research attempts to understand the significance of the facts. It attempts to discover and explain patterns, regularities, and relationships. It seeks prediction based on understanding. In addition to using techniques of data collection, the scientist also works with concepts, principles, hypotheses, models, and theories. Of these, theory is one of the most important but frequently the least understood. The naturalist does not focus his attenion on theory, so vital to the scientist and through which science makes some of its principal contributions to knowledge.

The scientist, if he is successful in studying facts, will develop knowledge which will increase his understanding, and from a practical standpoint, make it possible for him to predict results to be expected under a given set of circumstances. It is true that fact gathering can make possible some predictions, but it is prediction without understanding. It is similar to using rules of thumb. Following detailed observations of birds, the ornithologist can predict the migration of birds in the fall of the year. The astronomer can also predict the movement of celestial bodies but his predictions will be more rigorously founded than those of the naturalist. The astronomer's predictions will be supported by well-established theory and by very precise mathematical models. His predictions will be supported by a much higher level of understanding than will those of the ornithologist. The ornithologist really does not have a very good explanation for the flight of the birds south, whereas the astronomer, in comparsion, has a very good explanation of his observations. Physicists and chemists similarly have a greater understanding of their subject matter. Fact gathering alone on supermarkets can provide some information in predicting the success of a particular store, but the prediction is not as soundly based as it would be if the facts were supported by established theory.

It is important to point out that moving from one level of understanding to another is moving along something like a continuum. The naturalist has some understanding of his phenomena, but it is not at the same level as that of the physicist. The argument that fact gathering and scientific research are not really levels of distinction but degrees of understanding might possibly be answered in the affirmative. This, however, is not the point to be made in attempting to make research—in this case, business research—scientific and vigorous. The point is that research efforts should seek to go as far as they can toward achieving the goal of scientific analysis and explanation.

Orthodox business research has not gone as far as it could. In its great emphasis on fact gathering and interpretation, it has overlooked the work of studying facts scientifically and the development and use of concepts, theories, and models to explain the patterns revealed by the facts. Traditional business research has not been critical of the concepts it has used in gathering facts. It has not emphasized the search for meaningful theories to guide research or the task of developing and testing hypotheses. It has not sought to develop new or improved solutions to significant operational problems. Too long has it played the role of the naturalist, the recorder of facts, and concentrated on sources of information and techniques for gathering data.

The failure of traditional business research to emphasize either the development or use of theory and hypotheses has been a serious weakness. It has not contributed significantly to basic knowledge or to the development of new or improved solutions to operational problems. In its reporting, it has failed to evaluate critically the facts to be gathered, and hence data collected were not always pertinent. One role of theories and hypotheses is to guide fact gathering. Usually, the argument supporting the set of facts to be collected is not based on theory or hypothesis but rather on some hazy notions or according to the apparent demand for the facts. The evaluation of the facts to be collected may be similar to that made by the census in deciding on what data to collect—those for which there seems to be the greatest demand or use. When understanding is limited, fact gathering may have to rely on hazy notions but every effort should be made to base fact gathering on as sound a theoretical foundation as possible. The interpretation of the facts collected is at best sketchy, vague, and limited.

NEW CONCEPT OF BUSINESS
RESEARCH: SCIENTIFIC RESEARCH

There can be no argument with the professional manner with which traditional business research has collected facts. Great precision has been achieved to insure the accuracy of statistical surveys and computations. This professional manner, however, has not been enough. Intellectually, business research has been passive. The new concept of business research which is finding its way into the firm and the university is drastically altering this picture. Modern business research integrates fact gathering with theory and with techniques of analysis to depict patterns, relationships, and regularities. It incorporates the use of models and mathematical techniques. The studies are more vigorous and disciplined than those of traditional business research. It is making important contributions to improving problem solving and to the growth of theoretical knowledge in the various fields of business administration. It is conducting all the many types of research which Francis and Brown include in their various classifications, plus applied research to develop new or improved solutions to significant operational problems.

These efforts have developed virtually a new language and a new body of knowledge. The program of an annual meeting of the Institute of Management Science provides an interesting study in this new language of the new body of knowledge which has been developing during the last ten to fifteen years and which is working a revolution in business research. For example, the titles of the various sections of the conference used such terms as Decision and Network Models, Accounting and Value Theory, Simulation Methods, Queuing Theory and Systems Engineering, Resource Allocation Models and Programming, Games, Decisions, and Strategies. Some of the papers discussed developments in the new knowledge under these titles, "Recent Developments in Stochastic Decision Theory," "Accounting, Management Science, and Business Decision Making," "Large Scale Economic Decision-Making Models," "Dynamic Models and Analogies in the Study of Large Scale Systems," and "Multi-Stage Programming Models."

This language, which is also appearing at other professional meetings dealing with business problems, is quite new to most businessmen and professors in colleges of business administration and is, in truth, a new language to them. It is meaningful to a relatively small group of people but this group is growing rapidly, especially in the large corporations and universities where the pioneering work is still being done. A few basic terms in this new body of knowledge, which is as yet not well defined, are becoming widely known but are only vaguely understood or are loosely interpreted. Examples would include "operations research," "motivation research," "linear programming," "statistical decision," "cybernetics," "simulation," "heuristic problem solving," "stochastic models," and "managerial economics." As some readers will recognize, these terms appear in different disciplines and fields, but all have appeared rather recently and may be considered a part of the new knowledge, since they are so often closely related in solving business problems.

Like many innovations, an interesting aspect of this new knowledge is the fact that much of it is not new. Some of its techniques are quite familiar. Operations research, for example, relies heavily on well-known statistical methods. Motivation research has come from psychoanalysis and the ideas introduced by Sigmund Freud. Managerial economics is closely related to the theory of the firm and statistical analysis. The basic novelty in the new approach to business research is the emphasis on scientific thinking.

One of the most promising aspects of the recent developments in business research for the discipline of business administration is the fact that they have concerned themselves with basic research as well as applied research. Although the efforts in the area of applied research, such as the work in operations research, are better known and have received more recognition, significant studies are under way that are concerned with basic research. The results of this work include, for example, theoretical work on how decisions are made in organizations.

Undoubtedly, the impact of scientific research on business administration will be revolutionary because of its great potential for solving problems in business. It will greatly enhance the effectiveness of management and, in the process, will alter the role of various levels of management and change the operating pattern of organizations. It will improve the understanding that society has of business. Business research is becoming a scientific activity.

2

Scientific Thinking

The scientific method has been developed over the centuries for systematically increasing knowledge, and although it certainly is not the only means for increasing knowledge, it has proven to be one of the most effective. The great strides in human understanding and technological development taken by man during the last three to four hundred years were made possible primarily by scientific research. Modern industrial civilization is built upon the knowledge this method has produced.

Sometimes the scientific method is confused with tools and techniques which it uses, such as the experiment, the random sample, and particularly hypotheses testing. It is, however, itself a constantly growing body of knowledge which among other things, guides and controls the use of tools and techniques. For someone either to appreciate or engage in scientific research, it is as important—if not more important—to understand this method as it is to grasp the techniques and tools it uses or the knowledge which it produces.

CONCEPTS AND SCIENTIFIC RESEARCH

Basic building blocks of scientific investigation are concepts. Whether the subject of a study is an esoteric one such as the treatment of the businessman in novels or the solution of the very practical problem of budgeting expenditures, careful attention must be given to concepts, because they are fundamental devices for thinking about phenomena. Through them we can

12

organize our experiences and observations. Without them there is virtually no thought; and conversely, as the individual increases his fund of concepts, his ability to think about his environment will tend to grow.

Obviously, concepts are not "basic to scientific method alone: *they are the foundation of all human communication and thought*. Since, however, science requires a greater precision in communication, the process of conceptualization must be much more consciously a part of science than is the case for most common-sense and everyday contexts." [1] Furthermore, the process is especially important to science because concepts provide the basic orientation for research. The set of concepts used determines the success or failure of a study. An appropriate set of concepts can be most helpful in the study of a phenomena and a new concept can result in a significant scientific breakthrough. An unsatisfactory set of concepts can result in failure even though the tools and techniques might have been very effectively used. Because of their importance in research, concepts are themselves a legitimate field of investigation and study.

Simple illustrations can give some insight in the role of concepts. For example, the individual can be thought of as an employee, a student, a taxpayer, or a parent. Each of these concepts suggests a different orientation for the study of the individual. Thinking of a person as an employee suggests a different set of questions to ask than thinking of him as a student. The business firm can be thought of as a method for organizing production or as an opportunity for investment. A third possibility is to think of it as an established system of communication. Each of these three viewpoints suggests different forms of analysis and different sets of data to collect. Whether we have one or several concepts for regarding the business firm, most of us do have a method available for thinking about it. A young child, on the other hand, typically has no concepts for regarding the business firm. It is beyond his thought process. The best that he may be able to do is think of it as adult activity.

Illustrative of efforts to find satisfactory concepts for investiga-

---

[1] William J. Goode, and Paul K. Hatt, *Methods in Social Research*, McGraw-Hill Book Co., New York, 1952, p. 43.

THE HUNT LIBRARY
CARNEGIE INSTITUTE OF TECHNOLOGY

tion has been the research on economic growth. It is one of the more fluid topics in economics and one of the reasons for its fluidity has been the difficulty in establishing a satisfactory set of concepts for thinking about economic development. W. W. Rostow in his book, *The Process of Economic Growth*,[2] suggested five concepts for analyzing economic growth: the traditional society, the preconditions for takeoff, the takeoff, the drive to maturity, and the age of mass consumption. Within the framework of these concepts, Rostow explained economic growth. W. Arthur Lewis in *The Theory of Economic Growth* [3] talks about the will to economize, economic institutions, knowledge, capital, population and resources, and government. These concepts provide quite a different framework from those of Rostow. Other students of economic growth have suggested alternative concepts. This fluid condition in the study of economic growth is in marked contrast to that of traditional economic analysis of the market economy which has adhered rather closely to the concepts of price theory. Economics, however, lacks the stability that we find in a field such as physics, where concept development has been refined to a very high degree.

The need for satisfactory concepts to guide research was brought to the author's attention recently by a proposed research project which emphasized studying the behavior of groups of five or six people who were working as a committee to solve problems of the business firm. The members of the research group had taped the discussion of several groups and were preparing to analyze the material. The problem was to decide what should be observed; that is, what concepts were pertinent—type of question asked, length of discussion before decision, group organization, and so on. Members from different disciplines tended to note different behavior as they listened to the tapes and there was no agreement on what was worth noting. It became evident that if the study were to be successful, the researchers would have to

---

[2] W. W. Rostow, *The Process of Economic Growth*, W. W. Norton and Co., New York, 1952.
[3] W. Arthur Lewis, *The Theory of Economic Growth*, Richard D. Irwin, Homewood, Ill., 1955.

interrupt their work and devote considerable time to developing a satisfactory set of concepts.

Concepts are inventions of the human mind to provide a means for organizing and understanding observations. They are not discoveries. The concepts of price, credit, debit, and employee were not discovered any more than were such things as automobiles, accounting techniques, or assembly-line balancing methods. We may discover items in the environment to which we attach concepts, but we do not perceive the concepts. We invent them. For example, we discover something and then invent concepts such as dirt, soil, ore, and loam for thinking about what was discovered. Each of the concepts provides a different way for thinking about that which was discovered. Concepts, therefore, are not the same things as the phenomena being observed.

It is sometimes forgotten that concepts are logical constructs created from sense impressions, percepts, or even fairly complex experiences. The tendency to assume that concepts actually exist as phenomena leads to many errors. The concept is not the phenomenon itself; that is, such logical constructs do not exist outside the stated frame of reference. The failure to recognize this is termed the *fallacy of reification,* that is, *treating abstractions as if they were actual phenomena.* This is such a common error that most of us are occasionally guilty of it.[4]

Remembering that concepts are inventions and not part of the environment being observed focuses our attention on the flexibility in the choice and use of concepts in research. If an invention such as an automobile proves unsatisfactory, it can be changed and altered by additional inventions. Similarly, if the concept, marginal cost, proves unsatisfactory we can also alter and change it by additional inventions.

Inventing (or borrowing) a concept provides a new way of thinking about phenomena. The shift from the concept that the world is flat to the idea that it is round suggests a very different way for regarding or thinking about our environment; such a shift led to the conclusion that we should be able to travel around the world without falling off and hence discover what

---

[4] Goode and Hatt, *op. cit.,* p. 42. (*Methods in Social Research,* 1952, McGraw-Hill Book Company, used by permission.)

was on the other side. This new concept revolutionized the way people thought about ocean travel and eventually revolutionized travel. (It is interesting to note that the concept of flatness is still useful to some navigators. The average motorist, using a road map from his local service station, in effect plans as though the route over which he will travel is flat. For him to think in terms of roundness would unnecessarily complicate his travel planning.) Another historic shift in thinking took place when people changed from considering the world to be the center of the universe with everything revolving about it to one where the earth was one of many bodies in a system in which the various bodies revolve about one another.

Introducing the concept of leadership suggests a particular way for thinking about human behavior. It suggests something to look for when observing a group. Without this concept, we may observe the group in some other fashion: for example, size, adherence to customs, noisiness, and age. Tradition is another concept which suggests something to look for when observing the behavior of a group. A third concept would be group leadership tradition.

The possibility of inventing concepts provides the opportunity for developing different ways for thinking about the same phenomena. Total cost, average cost, and incremental cost each suggest variations for regarding phenomena. The phemomena does not differ—only the way of thinking about it differs. The economist and the sociologist have different sets of concepts which will lead them to observe the same phenomena differently and hence collect different data. The existence of different concepts for considering the same phenomena can help to explain why people can differ so widely in opinion concerning some subject of common interest such as politics, economics, and religion. The same phenomena will be observed differently, and people will interpret or understand the same observations differently.

The process of inventing concepts is an integral part in the growth and development of a discipline (or field). It is a complex process analogous to creative thinking and innovation in literature and the fine arts—drama, music, and sculpture. In the early stages of its growth, a science will use concepts borrowed from conversational language but, before long, find that these are inadequate. Such borrowed concepts will not be sufficiently precise; they may involve ambiguities; and most important, they may simply not be appropriate. The science will then seek to refine or introduce new concepts. In the process of being analyzed, these concepts may be broken down into more than one concept. Gustav Bergmann cites an example of this pattern in his book, *Philosophy of Science:*

Take "force." For a long time now in mechanics it has served as an abbreviation for the product of mass and acceleration and for nothing else. This was not always so. At an early stage, in the eighteenth century, the term was still used ambiguously or alternatively for the three different things that are now called force, momentum, and kinetic energy . . . There was even some discussion then, among very distinguished men, about which of the three was really "force." [5]

An example of a term in business and economics that has been broken down into several concepts is "capital." Instead of "capital" other terms are frequently used—net assets, equity, producer goods, investment funds. Debates over the meaning of "capital," like "force," have to some extent been resolved through new concepts which constitute inventions and are the product of innovation and creative thinking.

Sometimes the adoption or invention of a new concept can dramatically reorient a discipline. This happened to physics when Einstein introduced the concept of "relativity." Accounting was drastically changed by the introduction of the idea of double-entry bookkeeping. The idea of marginal analysis formed the basis for modern economic thought and was almost as important to it as relativity to modern physics.

Eventually, as a discipline develops, the connection between its technical language and that of conventional conversation becomes quite distant. Highly specialized concepts are developed. They may be given labels which are used in everyday conversation or they may be given special terms. Where new concepts are developed but given labels from general conversation, difficulties typically develop. Economics offers an excellent example of this problem. Many terms in economics have a technical meaning

---

[5] Gustav Bergmann, *Philosophy of Science,* University of Wisconsin Press, Madison, Wis., 1957, pp. 48–49.

quite apart from that of conversational language. It may sometimes be better for a science to develop new terms for a new concept which it develops, rather than to continue to use terms taken from conversational language. One advantage of using symbols instead of words to refer to a concept is the ease of avoiding confusion with concepts of general conversation. Inventing new words, on the other hand, can mean new labels without either new concepts or any concepts at all. This practice of labels without concepts—words without meaning—is often referred to as jargon. It can slip into scientific writing when the writer has deluded himself into thinking that the new term is associated with a new concept.

The progress of a discipline in increasing its knowledge can go only as fast as the science is able to develop effective and satisfactory concepts for regarding its area of interest. Concepts which are fuzzy, ambiguous, or inappropriate will prevent not only satisfactory observation but also clear thinking. Because of the important role which concepts play in a discipline, they provide a significant clue to understanding it. They form a special language to be learned if the science is to be understood.

Accounting and economics offer excellent examples illustrating the development of a fairly elaborate set of concepts and hence technical language. Physics and chemistry offer even beter examples of complex concepts and terminology. On the other hand, somewhat newer areas such as management, which are seeking to formalize their study of a specific subject matter, have not developed as technical a language. Their concepts are still quite close to those of conversational language and, consequently, are not as well defined nor as useful as those of the better developed disciplines. This does not, however, mean that the newer disciplines have not developed some rather useful concepts.

CONCEPTS IN CLASSIFICATION AND OBSERVATION

One of the most obvious advantages provided by a set of concepts to a discipline is their service as a tool in the collection and classification of data. Concepts if well defined can place in the hands of the researcher a tool to guide his observations and a scheme which he can use to classify the information collected.

The concepts of height and weight provide the anthropologist with two tools which he can use in observing and classifying people. A somewhat more sophisticated concept of the anthropologist is the cephalic index, a number obtained by dividing the maximum breadth of the cranium by its maximum length and multiplying by 100.

The naturalists have, over the years, developed very detailed conceptual schemes which have provided them with a most sophisticated classification system to guide them in their work of observing and classifying natural phenomena. One of the basic tasks of the naturalist is to attempt to discover all types of living creatures, observe them, and fit them into a classification pattern. He is concerned with insuring that his conceptual scheme will include a logical pattern for all the creatures he observes. A discovery for the naturalist takes place when he finds a new type in an old pattern or discovers a brand new pattern. A new type in an old pattern would be, let us say, a new type of dog never before observed. A new pattern would be an entirely new type of creature which does not seem to fit into any existing family classification.

The ornithologist's work is typical of a naturalist. He has classified birds according to orders, families, and subfamilies. He has attempted to make his classification system comprehensive enough to include all birds that have been observed. For each concept of order, family, subfamily, and so forth, he has prepared a technical definition with an effort to make it sufficiently clear to indicate where a particular specimen fits and also to guide someone who seeks to observe examples of the specimens. There are publications available for the bird watcher which are, in effect, special dictionaries with detailed definitions. In a geographic area that has been well studied, most birds observed will readily fit into a particular slot in the classification scheme. A discovery for the ornithologist takes place when a type of bird is observed that has never been seen before. It then poses the problem to the observer of deciding where in his classification scheme the bird should be placed: of what family it is a member, or whether it is a member of some as yet unobserved order or family of birds. If it happens to carry its young around in a pouch or is cold blooded, it would certainly start another classification system under the general category of birds or introduce a new category of flying creatures.

To appreciate the value of a conceptual scheme for observing phenomena and gathering data, we could compare the position of the novice, who knows very little about birds, with that of the ornithologist. The novice, when he walks forth into a field or through a forest, will be quite limited in making meaningful observations. Everything he sees that flies may be simply classified under bird. He may have a few crude categories involving color and size. He may exclude hummingbirds (considering them insects) but include bats as birds. The ornithologist has a more refined set of concepts and will, as a result, "see" more than the novice.

Another example would be to consider the plight of an early American Indian if he were to walk into a modern American kitchen. He would be quite puzzled by his observations. The refrigerator, stove, toaster, coffeemaker, blender, and garbage disposal would tend to be meaningless stuff in the environment. At best, they would be meaningful in a way quite different from ours. The stove might be thought of as some form of table and the blender as some type of container for holding fluids. Because the Indian did not have a concept or set of concepts suitable from our standpoint for the particular observations, he would have difficulty in understanding his environment and making meaningful observations. On the other hand, today's housewife is equipped with a conceptual scheme which includes a set of concepts for the various items found in the kitchen that would assist her to make meaningful observations. In the process of growing up and receiving an education in our culture, she learned a set of concepts which equipped her to organize and understand the observations made. They provide her with indications of what and how to observe in the kitchen. Conversely, the housewife, if placed in a forest, might find herself very limited in observing her environment compared with the Indian who might have a very complicated conceptual scheme of the forest. Both might find themselves equally mystified and unable to meaningfully observe if placed in an electronic computer laboratory.

These examples point out the requirements for successful observation and classification—having a conceptual scheme to fit the environment. Accounting provides such a scheme for classifying and recording the monetary transactions of the firm. The test of the accounting system in any particular situation is the extent to which it provides a classification system for all types of transactions that are observed. Because of the wide variety of transactions in the modern business firms, the accountant, like the naturalist, must have a very detailed scheme for classifying the transactions. As business practices and activities change, the classification system must adjust to handle new types of transactions that evolve. Hence, one of the functions of the accounting scholar, like that of the naturalist, is to be continuously on the alert to analyze the effectiveness of his classification system for handling new observations. An interesting problem in the education of accounting students is balancing the emphasis placed on learning how to use existing classification systems against learning how to modify existing classification systems when they prove inadequate.

Critical to a conceptual scheme designed to classify data is the availability of definitions which will provide satisfactory rules and procedures for identification of observations. The accountant, for example, must begin by making quite clear what is to be a debit and a credit. He must then under each of these broad categories provide definitions for the subclasses under debit and credit. The Bureau of the Census, in its decennial tally of the population, goes forth each ten years armed with a set of carefully defined concepts for counting and classifying people into a variety of categories such as residence, education, and occupation. Since there are so many people and categories involved in taking the census, it is vital that the definitions be quite clear to insure the comparability of data collected throughout the United States.

PATTERNS, REGULARITIES AND RELATIONSHIPS

Notwithstanding how elaborate, how sophisticated, how well-defined a concept or set of concepts, a fundamental question, left unanswered by the mere existence of a concept or set of concepts, is the significance or importance of these concepts. Of what significance are the concepts of opportunity cost, staff, line, broker, per capita income, and unit cost. Ease of definition and value in classification do not alone establish importance. We can readily think of many concepts which could be quite easily defined and used to classify. A concept can be suggested which may be defined in terms of the number of pennies which enter a cash register per hour. It can be used to collect and classify data but of what value is the concept? The natural historian may be satisfied with data collection and classification, but the scientific investigator wants more. He wants understanding and prediction. The interest of a concept to him lies in its value in helping to understand phenomena and to predict behavior.

The concept of average sale, used for classifying business firms' monthly sales, does not alone increase our understanding of the firm. If, however, it is considered in relation to another concept such as average cost per sale, the value of the concept may become significant. We may find, for example, that we can predict something about average cost per sale if we know something about average sales.

Concepts, therefore, become significant and helpful in understanding phenomena and predicting events as they are found to be related to other concepts. The concept age of the human being can become significant as it is found to be related to productivity. The average cost of living in a community is significant as it is related to income. Total sales can become a significant concept as it is related to profit.

The use by a discipline of concepts solely to guide observation and for data classification is an elementary stage in its evolution as a scientific study. It is a stage at which there will tend to be little understanding of the phenomena. If a researcher did nothing but classify business activity, he would not understand much about his subject. Understanding begins with the analysis of the observations made to determine what, if any, relationships or patterns prevail among the concepts used in gathering and classifying data. As this stage proceeds, concepts become meaningful, for they are found to be related to other concepts.

If a set of concepts, in addition to providing a means for classifying and collecting data, is accompanied by information on the relationships among or between the concepts, a very powerful tool has become available for understanding the phenomena involved. Let us go back to the housewife, the Indian, and the kitchen. In addition to a set of concepts that provide her with a method for classifying what she finds in the kitchen, she also has information on the relationships among the concepts which allow her to understand, predict, and manipulate. Similarly, the Indian in the forest not only has a classification scheme, but also some idea of relationships to be found within it.

The discovered relationships between or among concepts may tend originally in the development of a discipline to deal with rather simple and obvious ones. It would take no great analysis to observe that the flight of birds south coincides rather closely with changes in the seasons; that the number of customers tends to increase with a reduction in prices; or that the sale of some products fluctuates with the seasons. As a result of rather obvious discoveries, it is possible to predict with some degree of accuracy. Understanding is somewhat limited, however, and prediction may be little more than rule of thumb.

Gradually, however, additional relationships can be discovered eventually building up a complex body of knowledge, a chain of relationships. The knowledge about relationships which astronomy has today is a long way from simple prediction of full moons based on the twenty-eight day cycle. From the knowledge of relationships, we can derive rules and procedures for problem solving. The idea that marginal cost increases and marginal revenue decreases as production increases suggests that profits can be maximized at that point where marginal cost equals marginal revenue.

The study of relationships and the refinement of concepts often go hand in hand. The preliminary relationships discovered in the early stages of a science may have been found to exist among concepts which are not particularly well defined; and hence, the meaningfulness of the observed relationship will not be clear. Often, relationships are observed to exist between concepts which have been taken from the spoken language and are rather vague. It may, for example, be observed that capital generally increases when income grows. As the two concepts, capital and income, are analyzed the relationships observed may become more precise. For example, capital might be broken down into several concepts, one of which might be plant and equipment.

Income might also be broken down and yield, among several concepts, income saved. The relationship between income saved and the increase in plant and equipment might prove to be a more precise relationship than that between the two rather general concepts.

As the knowledge of a discipline grows, it becomes a rather complicated system of relationships. Economists have evolved a very complicated conceptual scheme for observing a specific aspect of society and have also discovered a complex pattern of relationships. Through concepts such as price and quantity, they have developed the concepts of supply and demand. They have discovered the pattern of relationships between price and quantity known as elasticity of demand or supply. By studying the relationship between consumption and income, they have developed the concept of propensity to consume; they have discovered relationships between propensity to consume, investment rates, production, and employment. The discovered relationships such as elasticity of demand are themselves concepts and may, in turn, be found to be related to other concepts.

FORM OF RELATIONSHIPS

Critical in the study of relationships between or among concepts is determining the form or pattern of the relationship. The accomplishment of this task underlines a significant distinction frequently drawn between the social and physical sciences. In marketing, for example, there seems to be sufficient evidence to indicate that there is a relationship between advertising and consumer purchases, but the form or pattern of the relationship is not clear. In physics, on the other hand, not only is there evidence of a relationship between a freely falling body and the earth but also for the form of this relationship under certain circumstances; we have discovered that an object falls at the accelerating rate of thirty-two feet per second per second.

Economists have done a great deal of work in attempting to determine the form of relationships which they have discovered. Analysis of the familiar demand and supply curves are typical of the attempt to indicate the form of relationships. As the price changes, in what way does the supply or the demand change?

Does a small increase in price result in a small decline in demand, a large decline in demand, or no difference at all? The term used to refer to the form of the relationship here is the "elasticity" of demand. In the area of cost, economists have attempted to determine the form of the relationship between production and cost. A familiar method to indicate the form of a relationship is to plot cost curves on a chart. The relationship may also be depicted through mathematical equations.

In the fields of marketing, management, and accounting, numerous relationships are apparent, but the forms of the relationships are not clear. Even though accounting has placed great emphasis on empirical data and various computations, it does not have very much information on the form of the regularities. There appear to be a number of relationships such as the one between the liquidity of the firm and its ability to do certain things, but the exact form of the relationship is not clear. The CPA is trained, when examining a set of books, to check for specific practices and make recommendations accordingly. His training and his recommendations are based on assumptions about the relationship between these practices and the reliability of the accounting records. Although there may be a fairly widespread agreement on the existence of the relationships, there will not be a great deal of information on the specific form of the relationship but only information on the general relationship. There appears, for example, to be a relationship between the way budgets are developed and their administration, but the exact form of the relationship is not known.

It certainly should be emphasized, at this point, that the lack of information on the exact form of a relationship or regularity does not prevent satisfactory prediction under a variety of circumstances. A hunter, although he does not know the exact form of the regularity regarding the behavior of animals or birds, can predict accurately enough for hunting purposes. A plumber may not know very much about the form of the relationship in electrolysis, but he knows enough to appreciate the fact that connecting different metals can result in speeded corrosion. Similarly, the business manager may not know a great deal about the form of many pertinent relationships, but he knows enough to make a wide range of satisfactory decisions. Scientific research, however, by determining the form of relationships makes knowledge more precise, which certainly can help the businessman in making decisions and solving problems. His predictions will be more accurate, reliable, and based on more understanding.

HYPOTHESES

A valuable convention used by science in exploring regularities is the hypothesis—the tentative statement a scientist makes when he believes he has discovered the existence of a relationship or relationships. His hypothesis constitutes a statement of the supposed relationship and may state the form of the relationship. After studying the seasons and the flight of migratory birds, the scientist may hypothesize that when it is fall, birds will fly south. In studying organizations, a scientist might come up with the hypothesis that as the hierarchial status of a position becomes vague, the person occupying the position tends to become frustrated. It will be noted that the two hypotheses just mentioned have the form, "if A then B," which is the usual form that hypotheses take. Often an hypothesis might be quite specific about the form of the relationship.

The term "hypotheses" is used to indicate that a statement of a relationship is considered to be tentative and one to be tested and proven. It really refers to an attitude toward or the status of a statement. This means that any statement, new or old, can become a hypothesis. A well-accepted statement dealing with relationships can become an hypothesis if it is decided to test it. Each time a student is asked to analyze the relationship between the' hypotenuse and the other two sides of a right triangle to prove the Pythagorean theorem, he is treating the theorem as an hypothesis. The physics student repeating the experiments of the great physicist is taking accepted findings and treating them as hypotheses. He hopes, like his predecessors, to confirm the relationships through his experiment.

Frequently, the word "hypothesis" is also used when questions of fact rather than relationship are involved. The statistician uses it in this sense. The classic situation is the test to determine whether or not a sample mean is representative of the universe, or if the sample means of two populations are significantly different. Marketing research often uses the term "hypothesis" when seeking factual information on customer behavior. The hypothesis may be to the effect that the majority of the customers prefer a specific brand. This would be a condition of fact, not relationship. Sometimes the distinction between these two uses of the term tend to blur. In this last example the study could investigate the proposition that, as certain circumstances are approached, customers will tend to increase their preference for the brand. We would then have a relationship, if *A* then *B*. This distinction between the two uses of hypotheses again emphasizes the distinction between fact gathering and a study of relationships. The one use of hypotheses seeks to deal with the problem of relationships, while the other focuses on just facts. Unless there is a statement to the contrary, the term "hypotheses" will be used here to refer to statements about relationships following the form if *A* then *B*.

GENERALIZING

Research to determine the form of regularities also attempts to determine the various circumstances under which discovered forms will prevail: for example, the extent to which a given relationship between cost and production may prevail in an industry; or under what circumstances the number of people that a person can supervise varies directly with the nature of the task being performed and the skill of the labor involved.

The scientist in studying relationships to learn whether a relationship is unique or if it prevails under other circumstances or between other concepts is attempting to generalize. Is the phenomena of an apple falling in a vacuum and accelerating at the rate of thirty-two feet per second per second true of all apples and of other falling items? If it is finally decided that the same relationship prevails, not only between all apples and the earth but between all solid objects and the earth, we would then be approaching a discovered relationship which is generally referred to as a law. In this case it turns out to be the well-known law of gravity. The concept of a law refers to a relationship that has been verified and which will always prevail under a given set of circumstances. The specific circumstances under which the law of gravity has been defined is the fall of an object in a vacuum at certain points on the earth. There has been sufficient evidence gathered so that there is a universally accepted agreement on the existence of this law under stated circumstances The physical sciences have many examples where discovered relationships have been given the classification of a law.

The more general the relationship discovered by the scientist, the more valuable it will be. An example would be found in moving from the statement that an object falling to the earth accelerates at the rate of thirty-two feet per second per second to the statement (Newton's law of gravitation) that two objects attract each other in proportion to the product of their mass and inversely to the square of the distance between them. This more general relationship includes the former plus many others, for example, objects falling on the moon.

The social sciences have not achieved the precision of the natural sciences in the discovery of relationships which can be referred to as laws. The famous law of supply and demand, for example, has been found to be more limited in its area of application than it was originally thought to be. Say's law was to the effect that if the price of goods and services offered for sale were allowed to find its own level in the market place, a price would always be found that would clear the market. If the supply of goods relative to demand were great, the price would fall and all the goods would be sold. If the supply were low relative to demand, the price would rise. In the early thirties, during the Great Depression, the supply of goods and labor was high relative to demand, but they could not clear the market at virtually any price. Because the social sciences have had limited success in discovering the form of relationships and the circumstances under which they apply compared with the natural sciences, they do not typically use the term, law. This also explains why they are not thought by some to be sciences. The social scientists are not able to state with a high degree of precision the relationships which will prevail under a given set of circumstances. The social scientist can say there is a relationship between advertising and consumer buying, but he cannot indicate very satisfactorily how general is the relationship or the form of the relationship.

In generalizing about a relationship, the scientist is taking a very interesting step which must be clearly understood. Generalizations are typically based upon empirical observations. Measures are taken and computations are made. The generalization, however, involves a leap from the hard fact to a generally agreed on statement which, however, is not the same as the hard fact. A decision must be made when a sufficient number of observations or a satisfactory observation has been made to justify a conclusion. The hard fact might be the specific observation that a radical political group grew in strength almost in direct proportion to increases in internal economic pressure or external political pressure. The generalization from this hard fact involves a leap from the fact to a generally accepted principle that radical groups grow in this fashion; however, the principle can never be regarded as identical with hard fact. Even if the generalization is called a law, the most it can ever be is a judgment or conclusion on which there is universal agreement. Often, the extent to which the generalization can be relied upon is so great that it is virtually the same as a fact, but it is never quite so. There is always the gap over which the inferences were made.

Generalizations should not be thought of as true or false, but rather we should think of them as applying or not applying under various circumstances. The generalization is a statement that science has concluded is worth making; but science also needs to indicate under what circumstances the generalization prevails, and under what circumstances it does not prevail. If we wish to use the words "true" or "false," it would be best to say that it is true or false that a certain generalization prevails under a given set of circumstances.

When a discipline has developed a set of well-defined concepts and has discovered the form of the relationships prevailing between or among the concepts, and has secured rather widespread agreement on its generalizations based on the discovered patterns, it has achieved a very high level of scientific accomplishment. It has developed a rather firm grasp of the subject matter. It has analytical content in addition to descriptive content. It has the kind of information which the naturalist or simple fact gatherer does not obtain. There is, however, still missing a significant aspect for full understanding. This is the development of an explanation for the form of the regularity which has been discovered and an explanation for the generalizations adopted. This is the role of theory, possibly one of the most misunderstood words and one of the most significant to the scientist.

THEORY

In conversational language, theory has a wide variety of meanings. Theory is used to suggest speculation or conjecture. It is also used to refer to an untested proposition. In this sense, theory is used interchangeably with hypothesis—when proven it becomes law or "fact." Theory is also associated with vagueness and impracticality. Typical of this attitude is the statement, "It's all right in theory, but it won't work in practice." Another such statement is, "It's too theoretical." Both of these statements imply that theory offers a procedure for solving a problem.

None of these notions expresses what the scientist means when he uses the word theory. He gives it a technical meaning which is quite different from the commonly understood meaning associated with the word.

Theory is designed to provide an explanation for phenomena and it seeks to do so in a very special way. It attempts to develop an integrated statement bringing together information that has been developed concerning the phenomena being explained by the theory. Typically, a theory begins with a series of statements or assertions which deal with a number of concepts thought or known to be related. An economic theory could begin with a series of statements setting forth the relationship between a group of economic concepts. These assertions are known as the axioms of the theory. From these axioms are deduced conclusions which are known as the theorems. The nature of the axioms of a theory might vary. The axioms could be laws that have been discovered and established by science. The conclusions or theorems are statements about relationships which can be considered hypotheses to be studied. They can also be used as the basis for prediction.

Bergmann has offered the following statements which suggest definitions of theory:

If there has to be a formula again, one might say that a theory is a group of laws deductively connected. More accurately, a theory is a group of laws, usually rather few, from which others, usually a larger number, have actually been deduced and from which one expects to deduce still further ones. The laws that serve as the premises of these deductions are called the *axioms* of the theory; those which appear as conclusion are called its *theorems*.[6]

A scientific theory consists of (1) axioms, (2) theorems, (3) the proofs of these theorems, and (4) definitions.[7]

The theories of geometry offer excellent illustrations of the component parts of a theory. In the first place, we have the basic concepts provided by geometry—points, lines, angles, triangles, and others. Then we have axioms stated in terms of these concepts. The axioms of geometry, it might be noted, come rather close to assumptions and are not laws. An example would be some of the statements about straight lines: if two divergent lines pass through a point, they will not meet. (The reader should note that technically this statement is not empirically based; since the concepts do not have operational definitions, there is no way to test the statement or axiom.) On the basis of its axioms, geometry then proceeds to deduce—or prove—theorems such as those dealing with parallel lines never meeting. A theory in economics would follow the same pattern. It would begin with concepts and axioms which may be accepted generalizations or assumptions. Theorems would then be deduced from the axioms.

The logic of theory is deductive and similar to that of the syllogism. If *A* equals *B*, and if *B* equals *C*, then *A* equals *C*. This is the logic of drawing a conclusion from several statements. It is somewhat different from inductive logic, which is concerned with generalizing from observations. Inductive logic would be interested in empirically testing to determine if *A* equals *B*, or if *B* equals *C*, or if in the conclusion *A* equals *C*.

The deductions of a theory for their value rely on the soundness of the logic and the axioms. If the axioms are not well-established generalizations, then the conclusions will suffer in their value. Now, it is true that the conclusions may prove satisfactory in prediction; but this does not necessarily improve the status of the axioms, and hence leaves the theory somewhat lack-

---

[6] Bergmann, *op. cit.*, pp. 31–32.
[7] *Ibid.*, p. 35.

ing. The conclusions are useful, as are rules of thumb, but the theory is unsatisfactory as a scientific explanation.

Part and parcel of a theory are the basic concepts which give the theories their orientation. These conceptual schemes provide the framework for integrating a group of laws or hypotheses, or both. The molecular theory of matter suggests that all matter is made of molecules. If the concept is accepted, any laws or hypotheses which have been developed concerning matter should be consistent with this idea and should fit into the framework provided. The theory that light is something that travels in straight lines suggests a way of regarding light and should explain existing knowledge about light.

The basic concept of a theory, like any concept, is an invention and is a particular way to regard a phenomenon. The basic concept or conceptual orientation provides a keystone or cornerstone of the theory and may be referred to as a principle or basic principle. These principles of theory introduce a rather comprehensive concept for considering some phenomena. The more general the principle, the more valuable—because it will deal with a wider range of phenomena. A rather comprehensive principle would be to suggest that the behavior of all inanimate objects is controlled by physical laws, which are subject to direct observation and testing. Such an explanation, if accepted, would put aside other explanations which might explain the behavior of inanimate objects in terms of devils, witches, and leprechauns. The explanation also suggests that if the investigator searches carefully, he should be able to discover the physical laws and the form of these laws.

Classical economic theory offered the principle that economic behavior could be explained in terms of the so-called "economic man," or in terms of the self-interest of the individual. This suggested the idea that if people were allowed to trade freely, prices would be determined by the bargaining of buyers and sellers and, that in a free market a price could be found that would clear the market. If there were a surplus of supply, the price would fall, and if there were a shortage, it would rise. In either situation a price could be found that would clear the market. Pavlov's concept that learning is conditioned behavior suggested a base for considerable work in theory in the social sciences. The innovation was the concept conditioned behavior. The concept of human behavior being determined by social norms has structured much of the thinking in the social sciences about human behavior.

According to Stephen Toulmin, principles or these underlying concepts of theory, constitute the basic discoveries of scientific investigation. In his book *The Philosophy of Science*,[8] he illustrates this idea using the discovery that light is something which travels in straight lines. He discusses the role of this discovery in changing the way light is conceptualized and points out that it formed the keystone to the theory of geometric optics. Toulmin points out that:

The discovery that light travels in straight lines was not, therefore, the discovery that, where previously nothing had been thought to be, in any ordinary sense, traveling, there turned out on closer inspection to be something traveling—namely, light: to interpret the optical statement in this way would be to misunderstand its point.[9]

The principle of a theory should be considered as a new concept and not the discovery of fact. As Toulmin indicated, the principle that light travels in straight lines represents a new way to think about light, and not the discovery of the fact that light travels in straight lines. This is a subtle point, but to go back to the discussion of concepts—we must remember that concepts are inventions of the human mind for regarding phenomena and this fact allows the same phenomena to be regarded in different ways. This fact also leads to the question concerning which of the various ways for conceiving some phenomena is the right one; the answer must be pragmatic. In effect, the conceptualization that is best or most appropriate is the one which gives us an approach to thinking about phenomena and leads to satisfactory explanation and accurate prediction. If we are traveling very short distances, it is quite satisfactory to think of the world as flat. If we are going around the world, this concept will leave something to be desired. This same test can be applied to the basic concepts of a

---

[8] Stephen Toulmin, *The Philosophy of Science*, Hutchinson's University Library, London, 1953. (Published by Harper and Row, 1960, by agreement with original publisher.)
[9] *Ibid.*, p. 20.

theory or to use Toulmin's language the principles of a theory. Do the concepts provide a basis for developing a framework which provides a satisfactory explanation of phenomena and allows for accurate prediction.

Facts should be distinguished from theory, because facts do not change. Iron rusts, water freezes, objects fall, and plants grow. The point of theory is to suggest a meaningful explanation for phenomenon through a conceptual scheme which brings together statements (axioms) from which additional statements are deduced. A new theory suggests a new way to look at old facts, but does not change them. Einstein's theory of relativity did not change the fact that objects in a vacuum on this earth fall at the rate of thirty-two feet per second per second. It did suggest a new way to regard the phenomenon. Keynes, in his *Theory of Unemployment*,[10] did not change the economic facts of the day but suggested that they be regarded in a different way.

Classical economic theory suggested that economic behavior could be explained in terms of economic self-interest and, therefore, suggested that economic activity should be studied within such a framework. Such an explanation suggested a study of prices, supply, and demand. It also suggested the study of influences which might interfere with the free exchange of goods such as by tariffs and monopolies.

A new economic theory might suggest that economic phenomena be regarded in a different way, and it might suggest new relationships. If a new theory suggests that economic behavior is not to be explained in terms of the so-called "economic man" but rather in terms of customs, traditions, and laws, it would suggest that in studying an economy one gathers information not just on prices, supply and demand, but also on a people's culture. This means that instead of just working out formulas showing the relationship between supply and demand, one may attempt to study the relationship between other aspects of a culture. It might even mean that trying to determine the pattern of relationships between supply and demand is not meaningful,

---

[10] John M. Keynes, *The General Theory of Unemployment, Interest and Money,* Harcourt, Brace and Co., New York, 1935.

and that other relationships might be more satisfactorily studied. The facts will not change but will be regarded differently.

Theory should also be distinguished from laws. Theory will not necessarily change discovered laws, but it will suggest that they be regarded differently. Theory might suggest a different explanation for a set of laws and suggest new relationships between laws. Laws will not be changed by theory, but reordered.

A distinctive aspect of theories is that they are a most dynamic phase of science and are really never considered completed or final. They are always held tentative, pending the development of a new theory which will provide a better explanation and a broader generalization encompassing more phenomena. The development of theory seeks to integrate more and more phenomena into a single framework. Keynes, in introducing his new theory, did not offer it as a substitute for classical economic theory but as a more general theory of which classical economic theory was a special case. Similarly, Einstein offered his theory of relativity as a more general theory of which Newtonian physics was a special case.

In evaluating a theory, one of the most significant questions to raise concerns how satisfactory a conceptual scheme it suggests for regarding phenomena. If a theory deals with concepts which are difficult to observe and for which it is difficult to secure data, it may be worthwhile searching for a theory that will provide a different conceptual framework. If a theory deals with concepts, empirical or otherwise, which are not well defined, the value of the theory will be limited. It may be a theory based on undefined jargon. The logic of a theory is another aspect from which to evaluate theory. Is the logic valid or are the deductions unwarranted? As has already been suggested, we may also question the premises, axioms, or assumptions of a theory from which theorems are deduced. Have these assumptions been empirically verified in any way? How well justified are they? Yet other questions to be asked are: How well does a theory explain existing knowledge? In what ways is it inconsistent? Of immense importance to research, does theory suggest new areas for research? Does it suggest new facts to gather and new hypotheses to test? Lastly, is the evaluation of a theory as a predictive device.

It has been mentioned earlier that the social scientists and students of business have not been as successful as the physical scientists in achieving precision in their knowledge. Specifically, they have not had the same success as the physical scientists in determining the form of the regularity. It may very well be that the social scientists and particularly students of business have not done enough work at the level of theory and on the development of conceptual schemes. Significant innovations offering new principles for regarding phenomena can suggest new concepts which can be more effectively defined than many that are presently being used. This can lead to new approaches to gathering facts and to more satisfactory research on the form of regularities discovered within conceptual schemes and the development of better theory. Such significant breakthroughs do not come along very often nor can they be programmed, but emphasizing research on theory can create conditions conducive to such developments.

3

Research in Problem Solving
and Decision Making

DOMAIN OF MODERN BUSINESS RESEARCH

Scientific research in business administration, as in any other field, is the use of the scientific method to study phenomena considered to fall within the domain of the discipline. Its function in business administration is, therefore, as broad as the discipline itself. Whatever problems or whatever phenomena fall within the domain of business administration are legitimate subjects for business research:

Development of new accounting techniques for handling depreciation.

Explaining the behavior of business executives in making decisions to invest in new productive facilities.

Devising a method to increase the effectiveness of advertising.

Explaining trends in the architecture of new banks.

Analyzing an innovation in business practice.

Testing a hypotheses which gives the relationship between budget methods and departmental behavior in forecasting and making expenditures.

Devising a method for negotiating labor contracts.

Developing a method to motivate employees.

Explaining the effect on authority of a new data processing system.

Inventing a technique to measure the cost of operating a service department.

The broad scope of modern business research includes using the scientific method to accomplish two fundamental objectives: to solve operating problems and to explain phenomena. These are two very different objectives which should be fully understood, not so much because of what or how the research is done but because of why it is being done. In the list of examples given above, note that some of the activities have rather "practical" objectives which appear to emphasize the solution of an operating problem rather than the increase of knowledge or understanding. The criteria of accomplishement in these studies will tend to be the success with which the problem is solved rather than the contribution to understanding phenomena, which is a secondary objective. It is not primarily concerned with developing laws, theories, and concepts. This type of research is classified as "applied research." The other activities in the list may seem, perhaps, to be somewhat esoteric: they might be of interest, but there is no apparent "practical" use for the information which the studies might produce. These studies seek to increase understanding, and the criteria for their success is the extent to which they are able to develop an adequate or satisfactory explanation. This is "basic research."

Applied research is prescriptive. It prescribes procedures or techniques for solving operational problems or offers solutions to the problems. This type of research is frequently thought of as problem-solving research. Anyone who seeks to solve a problem and make a decision engages in this type of research, whether he does it scientifically or not. Modern business research would apply the scientific method to problem solving. If we are faced with the task of introducing a new product or developing a new accounting method, scientific research would seek to do this scientifically. Although applied research does not necessarily increase our understanding of phenomena, it may do so as a by-product of its principle objective. The objective of basic research, also known as pure or fundamental research, is the development of knowledge which will increase understanding of phenomena being studied. It is not primarily concerned with prescribing methods to solve operating problems or solutions to those problems. Such information, if developed, would be considered a by-product. Basic research on personnel promotion practices would not be designed primarily to help industry improve its methods. Rather, it would be concerned solely with an analysis to explain the nature of the phenomena. It might, for example, develop a theory showing that a trend to emphasize seniority and to de-emphasize ability progresses with the age and size of an organization, or it may explain the process through a theory indicating that promotion is a function of efforts to bring about conformity and reduce unconventional behavior. Applied research, on the other hand, would undertake such a project in order to determine the most efficient way to promote people so as to select the best people without appreciably reducing organization morale.

The difference in basic and applied approaches, it should be emphasized, hinges on the objectives and goals. Applied research is concerned with objectives to manipulate things and people. It is operationally oriented. Basic research seeks to stand aloof from these objectives. Its sole concern is providing an explanation that will allow us to better understand phenomena.

Basic research and applied research do frequently converge. Applied research often finds the discoveries of basic research to be most helpful. For example, basic research may find that an individual's productivity tends to rise as he becomes able to identify with the goals of the organization. This development may suggest to the applied researcher who is seeking to raise productivity that a technique be devised to increase employees' identification with the organization's goals. The idea is basically a simple one. The discovery of a relationship between two variables by the basic researcher will suggest to the applied researcher that by manipulating one variable he can control the other.

On the other hand, applied research can also make a contribution to basic research. An applied researcher seeking to solve a certain problem may decide first to study the nature of the phenomena to determine the relationship between variables. In doing this, he will be accomplishing very much what the basic researcher does. Once he has discovered a relationship, he can then proceed to see if he can devise a method for controlling one variable in order to manipulate the other. In seeking to discover a formula for locating a bank, an applied researcher may first see if he can discover the relationship between bank location and customer behavior. If he then finds a relationship between customer behavior and the proximity of the bank to a shopping center and the customer's home, he will have some clues for the location of banks. At the same time, he may have to come up with an explanation for the success or failure of existing banks.

Since basic research and applied research can (and frequently do) perform the same things, their only real difference is in their objectives—which may seem a difference hardly worth emphasizing. The purpose in emphasizing this difference, however, is to underline the implications which the two objectives can have for the kind of research which will be done and the potential contribution which will be made. The distinction does not seek to place a value judgment on either—to infer that one type of research is more scientific than the other, or that they use different methods and techniques, or that one is more valuable than the other. Both can be equally scientific, both can use the same methods and techniques, and both are certainly important.

Anatol Rapoport, in commenting on Russell Ackoff's book *Scientific Method: Optimizing Applied Research Decisions*,[1] emphasized the importance of this distinction between applied and basic research. The methods and techniques discussed in Ackoff's book can be used both in applied and basic research, but as Rapoport pointed out, the book's orientation is toward applied research.

. . . definitely slanted to the decision maker, the man of affairs, the manipulator of men, machines, and resources. The Epilogue (Chapter 15) puts science into a broader social context, and, of course, it should do so. The "decision maker" (businessman, administrator, even the military man . . .) is after all a human being, and there is no reason why this should not be pointed out to him together with some remarks on what it means to be human. However, the bulk of this book is not written from the point of view of the "humanities." The title does not say this. Therefore the preface should say it in no uncertain terms, namely, that scientific method is treated here from a certain point of view, where the point of departure is a "problem" defined in "what to do" terms. It is also advisable to let the reader know that there are other points of departure. Science emerged not only from technology and administration; it emerged from art and religion as well. There the

---

[1] Russell L. Ackoff, *Scientific Method: Optimizing Applied Research Decisions*, John Wiley and Sons, New York, 1962.

points of departure were not at all "problems" faced by "decision makers." Even though every intellectual itch can be interpreted as a problem, if definitions are stretched far enough, the motivations of Kepler, Newton, Darwin, Mendel, von Humboldt, Mendeleyev, Helmholtz, and Einstein were for the most part not the *kinds of* motivations which are here taken as points of departure of scientific investigation.

As you point out, the distinction is not so much between "pure science" and "applied science." Pure science can certainly also be harnessed to problem-oriented motivations. If this is done, the distinction becomes only one between echelons in an organized enterprise. There is, however, a deeper psychological distinction which puts science into a dual role, namely, as a branch of the humanities and as an adjunct to technology. The tone, examples, the orientation of the volume are so definitely toward the latter aspect of science that it seems advisable to make an explicit acknowledgement of this slant. The frequently emphasized implications that science is power should be coupled with equally important reminders that science is also wisdom; i.e., avoidance of self-deception rather than a gain of control. I know the two are closely related, but there are also psychological distinctions between the two orientations which deserve bringing out.[2]

Basic research allows the investigator to conduct research free from the restriction to solve an operational problem. He is thus free to consider various viewpoints and concepts. He is free to follow ideas which may lead him quite far from his original point of investigation. Esoteric questions can be asked which may lead to apparently "irrelevant" knowledge with no "practical" use. The only justification he needs is whether or not he feels that he can increase understanding. This freedom is of incalculable value in efforts to understand phenomena. Without this freedom, efforts to build systematic knowledge to explain phenomena would be critically hampered. The unrestricted nature of basic research allows scientific inquiry to make rather extensive contributions to the enlightenment of man. Nagel mentions some of these benefits in the preface of his book, *The Structure of Science:*

Science as an institutionalized art of inquiry has yielded varied fruit. Its currently best-publicized products are undoubtedly the technological

---

[2] *Ibid.,* p. vii.

skills that have been transforming traditional forms of human economy at an accelerating rate. It is also responsible for many other things not at the focus of present public attention, though some of them have been, and continue to be, frequently prized as the most precious harvest of the scientific enterprise. Foremost among these are: the achievement of generalized theoretical knowledge concerning fundamental determining conditions for the occurrence of various types of events and processes; the emancipation of men's minds from ancient superstitions in which barbarous practices and oppressive fears are often rooted; the undermining of the intellectual foundations for moral and religious dogmas, with a resultant weakening in the protective cover that the hard crust of unreasoned custom provides for the continuation of social injustices; and, more generally, the gradual development among increasing numbers of a questioning intellectual temper toward traditional beliefs, a development frequently accompanied by the adoption in domains previously closed to systematic critical thought of logical methods for assessing, on the basis of reliable data of observation, the merits of alternative assumptions concerning matters of fact or of desirable policy.[3]

People with a primary concern for operational problems (people with a "practical orientation") will often express considerable annoyance with basic research because of its objective, and more specifically, with the results of its work. They are annoyed because the basic researcher and the results of his work do not prescribe solutions to so-called practical problems. In fact, basic research appears to have no value for the solution of an operational problem, and these people have difficulty in understanding the purpose of research that does not have such a goal in mind. They question the value of its apparently esoteric studies such as the Aztec's use of money or the social values of the modern executive. However, these people forget or simply do not understand that basic research not only can but does contribute to problem solving. It contributes through giving the problem solver a deeper and broader understanding of phenomena. Through its efforts to invent concepts and explore patterns, regularities, and relationships, basic research provides valuable clues to the solution of practical problems. It suggests new approaches

---

[3] Ernest Nagel, *The Structure of Science,* Harcourt, Brace and World, New York, 1961, p. vii.

to conceptualizing the problem and suggests the relationship to be expected between the concepts.

The contribution of basic research, however, is not always immediate or evident, which explains some of the frustration. It may take considerable insight sometimes to see the relationship between its discoveries and operational problems to be solved. By emphasizing basic research, however, science develops a store of knowledge, which becomes available for the solution of operational problems, and a store of knowledge which would not otherwise be developed. Without basic research, applied research might be little more than trial and error based on a frozen, rigid, and static understanding of phenomena. Although people in applied fields such as business and engineering may not themselves engage in or at least emphasize basic research, progress in applied research will depend on basic research in related areas.

THE PROBLEM-SOLVING PROCESS

Since business administration is an applied art, the principal concern of modern business research has been applied research to improve the efficiency and effectiveness of problem solving; and it has made significant progress leading to the solution or improved solution of a wide variety of managerial problems. It has developed techniques and prescribed solutions dealing with all aspects of the problem-solving process. It has emphasized the scientific method and drawn heavily upon the knowledge of related disciplines such as economics, statistics, and psychology.

The problem-solving process is a complex activity and offers a variety of opportunities to business research. Studies can deal with aspect of—or with—the whole process. Current applied research deals with both. This problem-solving process (see Table 1) can be thought of as having three basic activities, which can in turn be further divided. In the first phase, problem analysis, the problem is formulated and alternative courses of action are developed. In the second step, prediction, the probable outcome of the alternatives is predicted. In the final step, decision making, the most appropriate alternative or alternatives are selected.

Problem analysis is usually stimulated by information suggesting a need for action to alter or remedy a situation: profits are

TABLE 1   The Problem-solving Process

	Problem-analysis		Prediction	Decision Making	
	Operating system	System's environment	Theory	Goals in the environment	The decision
Stimuli	Problem formulation	Alternative courses of action $A_1, A_2, \ldots, A_n$	Prediction of alternatives	Evaluation of predictions	
	System's goals	Goals in the environment	Experience	System's goals	

declining, competitors are reducing prices, unit cost is increasing, new accounting methods have been developed, the value of company stock is declining, employee morale is sagging. This information, creating on the part of the decision maker a felt need for action, is analogous to symptoms of a disease and is typically not the problem but rather a manifestation of the problem. Just as an abnormal temperature in a person is not the problem but a symptom, so a fall in profits or rise in costs is not a problem but a symptom. The fall in profits may result from inefficient salesmen, product obsolescence, poor raw materials, or even inappropriate accounting. The basic skill of a good administrator, like that of a good physician, is that of being able to recognize symptoms and to either diagnose them or have them diagnosed.

The context for diagnosis of the stimuli, or in this case problem analysis, are in addition to the stimuli: the system, its goals, the system's environment, and environmental goals. The term system is used here to refer to the organization structure, or activity with which the decision maker is directly concerned as manager or administrator. In the case of a physician, the system with which he is directly concerned is the patient's body, its pattern of reaction to external and internal stimuli and its technique for controlling and directing its own activity. The environment of the body would include such things as the patient's working environment, his social environment, the life cycle of a parasite attacking the body, and the physical climate. In a manufacturing operation, the system would include production, planning, transportation, communication, recruitment, training, management, and whatever other activities may be involved in controlling and directing its operations. The system's environment would include the market, the national economy, labor unions, and so on. Both the system and its environment will provide the overall framework and the restrictions that structure and define the operating position of the decision maker. Aspects of the system's environment can, of course, also be thought of as systems; the market system and the economic system, for example. The broader term "environment" is used rather than the possible term "external systems," because not all of the external factors may be conveniently thought of as systems. Information triggering the problem-solving process is produced by both the system and its environment. Information produced by the system would include accounting, personnel, and production reports, while that produced by the environment could include data on competitors, new products, customer behavior, and new legislation.

The goals of the system are the various objectives—long range, intermediate range, and immediate range—which an organization seeks to accomplish and are essentially the basic aims of the organization. The long-range goals could include achieving a desirable profit return on investment and a given share of the market. The intermediate goals are concerned with shorter periods of time and are designed to lead toward the long-range goals. Examples would include specific projects that involve several months or years to accomplish such as adding a branch plant, introducing a new line of products, changing consumer attitudes, changing employee attitudes, or company reorganization. The immediate goals are concerned with day-to-day and week-to-week activities designed to carry out the intermediate goals: setting production schedules, controlling inventories, building a new assembly line, preparing advertising layouts. Long-range goals are almost synonymous with the overall orientation or basic philosophy of an organization—the fundamental reason for existence. Intermediate objectives are concerned with major steps to fulfill the basic philosophy; immediate goals, with the day-to-day steps to accomplish the major projects. Other possible analytical schemes can be used to consider goals. The basic thought here is simply to indicate a means-end chain in goal achievement. Environmental goals are objectives of systems found in the environment. From the viewpoint of the system, they may be conflicting, symbiotic, complementary or irrelevant. Included would be the goals of political, social, economic, or business systems.

The basic orientation for the means-end chain is the value system of the decision makers. This value system will be deeply rooted in the culture and the experience of the people in the system. It will depend on the customs, traditions, mores, and attitudes of the society in which they grew up plus the development of their personality. The value system is different from the goals themselves, but it provides a framework for structuring the means-end chain of objectives. It affects everything from the long-range goal of profits and community status to the organization's objective in the day-to-day treatment of employees.

The information which serves as the stimuli is analyzed in terms of the system, the system's environment, and the two sets of goals. The system can be studied to analyze the factors which are producing the information and, conversely, to consider the impact of the information. If the information indicates increasing average cost, the system can be studied to determine the factors that may be producing the increase. A new product can be analyzed in terms of the organization's market as well as its effect, if adopted, on the operation of the system. As the stimulus is understood in terms of the system and its environment, its significance can then be evaluated in terms of the two sets of goals.

Accompanying or following the evaluation of the stimuli will be the search for alternative courses of action which will resolve the problem. This will be a search for specific action that can be taken to solve the problem—hire a new sales manager, increase advertising budget 10 percent, introduce a new product.

For the alternatives to be meaningful, some prediction is needed to indicate the consequences or probable consequences that can be expected from taking the various available alternatives. It is then possible to attempt to select that alternative or group of alternatives that will most satisfactorily allow the accomplishment of the system's goals.

Prediction at the elementary level can be based on little more than rule of thumb or imitation of others. In setting an advertising budget, since it is so difficult to determine the consequences of various possible budget and media combinations, firms may use a rule of thumb to guide them in setting the budget—a fixed percentage of sales. The experience of others can be used as a guide: "Company X tried this approach in setting their budget, it seems to have worked, so let's try it."

Higher up the scale of sophistication is prediction based on previous trends. If a community's population has been growing for the last three decades, we may successfully predict that the trend will continue for the next few years. An empirical study may show that a filling station can be successfully located in a suburban area where the traffic count at the intersection reaches an average of X cars per hour, during the period from seven in the morning to seven at night. At the most sophisticated level would be the incorporation of theory to provide a basis for prediction. A theory of population growth could be used to predict population developments of a community. The theory will suggest the pertinent concepts and the relationships between them. The problem will then be to measure these concepts in the community and interpret the empirical data in terms of the theory.

The gap or space between experience and theory should most appropriately be thought of as a continuum; and the method of predictions will, in most cases, be a mixture of theory and experience. The prediction of the consequences in locating a supermarket at a particular site might be made in terms of theory and empirical experience developed by locating previous supermarkets.

Once the information has been developed to indicate the probable outcome of the various alternatives, the next step is decision making. This involves comparing the outcomes with the objectives so as to determine the alternative or set of alternatives which most satisfactorily accomplishes the desired objectives. This aspect of the process places a premium on the development of some technique which will make it possible to compare several alternatives or strategies with several goals, all of which the decision maker is seeking to accomplish. Life would be much simpler if there were, as a rule, only one goal to maximize; but usually there are several, and it becomes impossible to maximize any one goal. So the strategy developed is to try to come up with a decision that will give the most satisfactory overall gain but which may not maximize any one goal.

Business research to improve the problem-solving process can consider a wide variety of problems. It can develop techniques which deal with the entire process and develop a procedure for handling problem analysis, prediction, and decision. Another possibility is to focus on aspects of the process such as: securing information; analyzing the system, the environment, and goals; developing alternatives; predicting; or decision making. The studies could develop generalized methods for various aspects of the process or specialize methods suited to specific industries or fields in business administration—the oil industry, transportation, marketing, accounting, finance. Finally, business research instead of developing methods—could prescribe solutions to general or specific problems of an industry.

APPLIED RESEARCH ON THE TOTAL PROCESS

Research on the total process develops methods to improve management's general problem-solving capability. Simply suggesting the use of the scientific method, of course, accomplishes this. So does the proposal that problem solvers be both technically trained and broadly educated. The idea then is to devise an approach which attacks, in a single technique, all aspects of the problem-solving process.

One very well-known technique for accomplishing this broad goal is the development of materials for the case method of instruction. Another approach would be actual experience in problem solving. Neither of these approaches, however, is necessarily scientific and modern business research is seeking to improve upon them.

An interesting example of some recent studies that can be considered to deal with the overall process is the work of A. Newell, J. C. Shaw, H. A. Simon, and Fred Tonge. They have been exploring the development of heuristics for problem solving.

A *problem* exists whenever a problem solver desires some outcome or state of affairs that he does not immediately know how to attain. Imperfect knowledge about how to proceed is at the core of the genuinely problematic. Of course, some initial information is always available. A genuine problem-solving process involves the repeated use of available information to initiate exploration, which discloses, in turn, more information until a way to attain the solution is finally discovered.

Many kinds of information can aid in solving problems: information may suggest the order in which possible solutions should be examined; it may rule out a whole class of solutions previously thought possible; it may provide a cheap test to distinguish likely from unlikely possibilities; and so on. All these kinds of information are *heuristics*—things that aid discovery. Heuristics seldom provide infallible guidance; they give practical knowledge, possessing only empirical validity. Often they "work," but the results are variable and success is seldom guaranteed.[4]

Fred M. Tonge [5] applied this approach to assembly-line balancing. Alfred A. Kuehn and Michael J. Hamburger developed a heuristic program for locating warehouses.[6]

Another approach related to the case method and to actual experience, are the business games.[7] Business games simulate problem-solving situations that are thought to be typical of business and industry. The hope is that through the experience of playing the game the individual will improve his ability to solve problems and make decisions.

The value of business games as devices to improve decision making and problem solving is yet to be determined. The player does have to analyze problems, consider alternatives, and make decisions. He runs the gamut. Considerable controversy, however, has raged about the games. If interest and enthusiasm are to be considered the criteria, the games are certainly successful. But like many teaching devices, there is no reliable measure that can be used to study their contribution to improving problem-solving capability. The case method and actual experience suffer from some of the same limitations.

APPLIED RESEARCH ON ASPECTS OF THE PROCESS

To develop methods that deal with one or more aspects of the process, rather than the whole, is to assume that the various tasks of the process are sufficiently similar in enough instances to make finding generalized techniques to apply to them feasible and

---

[4] A. Newell, J. C. Shaw, and H. A. Simon, "Report on a General Problem-Solving Program," *Proceedings of the Internal Conference on Information Processing,* Paris, June 15–20, 1959, London; Butterworths, 1960, p. 256.
[5] Fred M. Tonge, *A Heuristic Program for Assembly Line Balancing,* Prentice-Hall, Englewood Cliffs, N. J., 1961.
[6] Alfred A. Kuehn and Michael J. Hamburger, "A Heuristic Program for Locating Warehouses," *Management Science,* Vol. IX, 1963.
[7] K. J. Cohen and E. Rhenman, "The Role of Management Games in Education and Research," *Management Science,* Vol. VII, 1961.

worthwhile. Examples of this research would include a generalized technique to produce information on the operating system or various elements in the environment, a method to analyze the operating system or its goals, an approach to prediction, and a method for decision making.

However, attention to the overall process could be eclipsed by such an emphasis placed entirely on the parts. This would bring to mind the adage about not seeing the forest for looking at the trees. The objective here is a consideration of the individual parts within the perspective of the whole process. This certainly is the frequently stated objective of operations research, which has done a great deal in developing methods for handling individual aspects of the process. It has sought to use these techniques within the framework of the system's operations and objectives.

An objective of O.R., as it emerged from this evolution of industrial organization, is to provide managers of the organization with a scientific basis for solving problems involving the interaction of components of the organization in the best interest of the organization as a whole. A decision which is best for the organization as a whole is called an optimum decision; one which is best relative to the functions of one or more parts of the organization is called a suboptimum decision. The problem of establishing criteria for an optimum decision is itself a very complex and technical one.[8]

Actually, the work of people in operations research can be thought of as dealing with both the overall process and with individual aspects of the process, with the emphasis on the latter. Examples of the former would be its suggestions to use interdisciplinary terms and the solutions of problems within the broad context of the operating system. Its primary efforts, however, have been to develop specific techniques which can be used to deal with one or more aspects of the problem-solving process.

Ackoff's *Scientific Method: Optimizing Applied Research Decisions*, like operations research, focuses on the overall task of improving management's capability to solve problems through methods which can be applied to individual aspects of the proc-

---

[8] C. West Churchman, Russell L. Ackoff, and E. Leonard Arnoff, *Introduction to Operations Research*, John Wiley and Sons, New York, 1957, p. 6.

ess. Within the following framework of problem-solving research, it discusses a number of generalized methods: [9]

1. Formulating the problem
2. Constructing the model
3. Testing the model
4. Deriving a solution from the model
5. Testing and controlling the solution
6. Implementing the solution

Management science like operations research, deals with individual parts of the decision-making process, but focuses on improving the overall system or at least it should.

As regards the foundation of "Management Science" the specifications are simple: to be meaningful, effective and useful "Management Science" should *focus on the definition of the characteristics of a business. Only when this job has been done (albeit crudely) should the analysis and the solution of individual operating problems be attempted.*[10]

Information Procurement. A key element in problem solving is securing information on the system and on the environment. Applied research can, therefore, study the process of making information available to decision makers and offers great potential as a field of study. In fact, this particular aspect of applied business research has been growing as fast as any other area. As might be expected, much of this research is emphasizing the function of the electronic computer in making information available. Some of it deals with methods for using the computer to provide existing reports more efficiently. Far more significant are the studies of comprehensive information systems to provide management with the knowledge it should have concerning the organization and its environment. This would incorporate more than data-processing techniques. After all, the new techniques can be used to handle existing data processing without necessarily improving management's information resources. The argument is that modern industrial structures are so large and complex that careful atten-

---

[9] Ackoff, Gupta, and Minas, *op. cit.,* p. 26.
[10] Peter F. Drucker, "Management Science and the Manager," *Management Science,* Vol. 1, No. 1, October, 1954, p. 125.

tion must be paid to the development of comprehensive methods to provide management with information on the operation of the system and on its environment.

New computers and other information-handling equipment are being perfected at a rapid pace, as are the new techniques of analysis and improvement which advance the quality of information that is produced and reduce the cost of producing it.

But, oddly enough, the rapid advance of technology, the abundance of new computers and new techniques, and the tremendous changes in the capacity and potential of new computers, all have been so intriguing that planning for their use has lagged. Nor has it helped matters that computers have become so complex that the very job of selecting one over another has been made difficult, especially in the face of an implied threat of 24-hour obsolescence. As a result, the ability of the average company to utilize the new computers and techniques falls far short of the potential the computer has to process the information necessary to operate the system.

. . . The majority of the systems-improvement programs we have studied resulted from method staffs having gone to work on a particular phase of the total system, such as payroll or inventory control. After this first phase was completed, a second phase would be tackled, then a third, and so on, until the program was completed. While substantial benefits may be derived from such an approach, the development of a master plan, like the one advocated here, can produce still better initial results and avoid costly replanning at later stages of the over-all program.[11]

In the article just quoted, the authors offer a broad solution which they feel will improve upon previous approaches to providing management with information. Also illustrating an attempt to provide a comprehensive approach to an information procurement is Adrian M. McDonough's book *Information Economics and Management Systems*.[12]

This chapter has considered certain problems of organization from an information point of view. It has recognized the growing emphasis on

---

[11] Marshall K. Evans and Lou R. Hague, "Master Plan for Information Systems," *Harvard Business Review,* January–February, Vol. 40, No. 1, 1962, pp. 92–93.
[12] Adrian M. McDonough, *Information Economics and Management Systems,* McGraw-Hill Book Co., New York, 1963.

management information systems in business and has sought to bring out both the merits and the difficulties involved. To be able to develop a formal arrangement for clarifying the problem-information structure of any organization, it is almost a necessity that some general set of classifications of management problems be available. The propositions for information management discussed in this chapter assume a degree of problem classification that does not as yet exist in most of our organizations. Our progress, however, is dependent on our abilities to spell out our problems, and this in turn means that we shall be increasing the resources devoted to problem classification.

In the following chapter a comprehensive scheme for classifying both management problems and associated approaches to solution is presented. As noted in Chapter 6, I have been working toward a definition of a field of knowledge—the field of management systems. The content of the next chapter represents an example of a scheme for assembling the scope and content of a large part of the knowledge associated with the problems of management. The retrieval system which is included provides the means for an initial attempt at structuring job modules by specific problem and knowledge elements.[13]

Problem Analysis. Satisfactory problem analysis, in effect information evaluation, requires an understanding of the operating system and the external environment of the system. Such an understanding is also important in the development of alternatives, in predicting, and in decision making. The significance of this problem is emphasized by the extensive work that modern business research is doing to analyze systems—all types. In fact the concept of system analysis has become fundamental in dealing with one or more aspects of problem solving and is a basic approach of operations research, which is sometimes thought of as system analysis.

This concept of system analysis has led directly into the technique of model construction of information systems, the whole or parts of the operating system, and of systems in the environment of the operating system. Model building makes it possible to depict regularities, relationships, and patterns in a system. It is a powerful technique which has proven most valuable in the physical sciences and engineering and is becoming increasingly useful in the social sciences. Its use has been developing rapidly in the

---

[13] From McDonough, *op. cit.*, pp. 144–145. Used by permission.

efforts of business research to improve managerial problem solving.

These techniques of model building, when used effectively, can be extremely helpful in understanding the behavior of a system and, thus, in formulating problems and predicting the consequences of an alternative course of action involving the system. Business research has been quite successful in developing techniques for building models of various aspects of the operating system and is currently experimenting with techniques for building models of entire operations, from the production line to the retailer. It has been most successful in building models emphasizing physical relationships rather than those involving human relationships.

A very ambitious effort to build models of operating systems is discussed by Jay Forrester in his book, *Industrial Dynamics*.[14] Mr. Forrester describes an approach which would encompass the entire operations of an industrial organization from the point of production all the way through to the retail outlet. The approach, which is highly empirical and considered by some to be antitheoretical, attempts to develop a model covering several years' operation and shows the relationship between a number of factors in the system. The model is designed to show how the effects of changed conditions—such as changes in orders or an increase in advertising—will affect the system. Mr. Forrester claims that industrial dynamics involves a dramatic breakthrough in industrial management of large organizations and will come into fruition within twenty-five years.

A specific example of a model of a system designed to predict courses of action was one developed by an electric utility system, which must make decisions not only from day to day but from hour to hour on the best combination of its production facilities to meet given patterns of supply and demand. If, for example, surplus power becomes available from outside the system, a decision has to be made whether or not to buy it and, if purchased, what steps should be taken within the system to absorb the out-

---

[14] Jay W. Forrester, *Industrial Dynamics*, published jointly by the Massachusetts Institute of Technology, Cambridge, Mass. and John Wiley and Sons, New York, 1961.

side supply. The problem is complicated because all of the system's generating units do not operate at the same cost, and they would not all be located near the entrance point of the surplus power. Through this model of the system decisions can be made to determine the most efficient combination of facilities.

The construction of models has been a basic tool in efforts to simulate a part or the entire operating system or some aspect of the environment. Forrester's model constitutes a simulation of an operating system. A large oil company has a simulation based on relationships between marketing, production, and finance. It was built to assist the company in making production and investment decisions. The business games mentioned above are based on mathematical models which seek to depict the relationship among concepts of the business firm and its environment.

Charles P. Bonini in his dissertation, *Simulation of Information and Decision Systems in the Firm*,[15] built a model to simulate the firm drawing upon theory from economics, accounting, and the behavioral sciences.

Using this model Bonini then tested several hypotheses dealing with the effect on the firm of changes in its external environment, its information system, and its decision system.

Determining Objectives. Another important area where research should improve problem analysis is the very difficult task of determining the objectives of the system and its environment. The job of discovering objectives is particularly complex when dealing with a large organization, where there can be so much conflict between its members. To develop methods that will be effective in determining objectives is important, because such goals provide a scale for the evaluation of the accomplishments or the prospective failures of the system. One approach to determine objectivies in an organization is through interviews with management. Motivation research and the depth interviews have added a dimension beyond the superficial questioning. Psychology, as might be expected, has done a great deal in this area.

In addition to determining objectives is the task of analyzing them. Research here would seek to study the relationship of

---

[15] Charles P. Bonini, *Simulation of Information and Decision Systems in the Firm*, Prentice-Hall, Englewood Cliffs, N.J., 1963.

several objectives. One possibility would be to consider the extent to which the accomplishment of one goal depends on accomplishing another. This would mean the establishment of means-end chains. Another problem is to measure the importance of the various objectives, so that they can be compared. Some objectives will have a higher value or utility to one person or organization than will others. This problem is also important in decision making, because it is a vital guide in attempting to select the most appropriate alternative to achieving the desired objectives.

Developing Alternatives. A final aspect of problem analysis is the development of alternative courses of action or, as sometimes referred to, developing strategies. Research on this problem would seek to increase management's ability to discover alternative courses of action to solve problems. An example of a superficial technique would be brainstorming, which prescribes that groups of people be given a problem, discuss it in a meeting, and then suggest as many solutions as possible—adhering to the one rule that no negative ideas can be introduced. An improvement over this approach is the idea suggested by operations research: the use of mixed teams drawn from several disciplines. The assumption is that people with different backgrounds will see the problem differently and hence suggest possible solutions that people from a single orientation might not otherwise consider.

Synectics, Inc.,[16] represents a group located in Massachusetts that has developed a research program to study human creativity and how it can be improved. Out of their work has come a course which they offer to improve creativity. Such a program, if successful, would certainly be a boon to problem solvers. Often the most difficult part of the process is simply the discovery of alternative courses of action, possible solutions to the problem.

The problem of developing alternatives is related to the processes of creativity and innovation. It is not the sort of thing which yields to formulas as readily as other aspects of problem solving, but providing conditions conducive to creative thinking and selecting people with potential for creative thinking suggests an approach to be used. The problem of bringing about creativ-

---

[16] William J. J. Gordon, *Synectics,* Harper and Brothers, New York, 1961.

ity has been of considerable interest to operations research and the following statement from Thomas L. Saaty's book, *Mathematical Methods of Operations Research*, states rather well the problem to be faced in developing creativity:

To develop creativity in an individual it is essential to encourage him from youth in habits of patient and independent thinking. This can best be accomplished in youth. Experience indicates that it is difficult to cultivate in the later stages of education the independence required for creativity; it must already be present. Without this independence the acquisition of facts and details becomes the goal of the mind, and their use is limited to established avenues of expression.[17]

Prediction. A most challenging opportunity for research is developing generalized models for prediction. The task of predicting the outcome or consequences of the various alternatives or strategies is an old one. Man, through the centuries, has been seeking to solve this problem. The construction of models and efforts to simulate phenomena illustrate efforts that can improve forecasting. Forrester's models, for example, would provide a method for forecasting. A study focusing on this aspect of problem solving is an extensive survey and evaluation of economic forecasting techniques by Robert W. Paterson.[18]

Decision Making. Once an effective method has been developed for predicting the results of alternative courses of action, the next step is to evaluate these alternatives in terms of the organization's goals and objectives and the selection of that alternative which will most efficiently lead to the desired objectives.

The problem is to devise a method to match the predicted outcomes against the desired goals. If the alternatives and goals are few, the decision function is simple, but as these components increase, the problem becomes complicated. The nature of the decision function can be illustrated below.[19] A_1 represents the

---

[17] From Thomas L. Saaty, *Mathematical Methods of Operations Research*, McGraw-Hill Book Co., New York, 1959, p. 383. Used by permission.

[18] Robert W. Paterson, *Evaluation of Economic Forecasting Techniques*, a Manuscript to be published in March or April 1965 by Center for Research, University of Missouri, Columbia, Mo.

[19] Russell L. Ackoff uses a very similar example in his two books, *The Design*

alternative to invest $100 in stock A_1, and A_2 is the alternative to invest the same amount of money in stock A_2. Q_1 represents the goal of getting a satisfactory return on investment, and Q_2 the goal of experiencing a market increase in the value of the investment. In Table 2, the amount on the left in each equation under the Q's represents the predicted result of each alternative in terms of the goals. (Investment A_1 will probably produce a return of $4.00 and probably experience an increase in market value of $3.00.) The second figure represents the value of the goals. As a prudent investor, you consider return on investment three times more important than increases in the market value, and hence you use 3 and 1 to weight the outcomes under Q_1 and Q_2 respectively. The final figure in each equation under the Q's represents the efficiency of each alternative to reach the particular goal. The total of the equations on the far right give a measure of the efficiency for each alternative.

TABLE 2

Alternatives	Goals		Evaluation of Alternatives
	Q_1	Q_2	
A_1	$4.00 × 3 = 12	$3.00 × 1 = 3	12 + 3 = 15
A_2	$2.00 × 3 = 6	$7.00 × 1 = 7	6 + 7 = 13

On the basis of these calculations, the alternative A_1 would be the most efficient approach to achieving the two goals Q_1 and Q_2.

Another aspect of this decision-making problem is to compare strategies between opposing individuals or groups. This would suggest a matrix comparing the strategies of two opposing forces. Instead of matching alternatives against goals, we could match alternatives of A against alternatives of B. Within the matrix we

of Social Research, The University of Chicago Press, Chicago, 1953, p. 32, and Scientific Method, Optimizing Research Decisions, John Wiley and Sons, New York, 1962, p. 32. In the latter book he describes it as an efficiency matrix. A variation of this scheme which incorporates probability is shown on p. 104 of Irwin D. J. Bross' book, Design for Decision, The Macmillan Co., New York, 1953. Donald J. Clough in Concepts in Management Science, Prentice-Hall, Englewood Cliffs, N. J., 1963, uses a similar scheme. His term is "the decision payoff matrix."

could enter the benefit to A or B or both. The task for A would be to pick the most appropriate strategy.

A classic example of decision-making techniques is the "diet problem." The diet problem is concerned with selecting those foods which will provide a minimum diet in terms of vitamins, proteins, and calories at the lowest price. The diet problem is an excellent example of a problem that lends itself to one of the most powerful techniques which has been developed in recent years, linear programming, which is being effectively applied to a wide variety of problems. Two other tools which have proven helpful in solving the decision functions are the theory of games and statistical decision. The theory of games, which is concerned with selecting strategies in competitive situations, is a dramatic development, but it is still in development stages, and its application to problem solving has been limited.

A great deal of the current work in modern business research has concerned itself with decision making. A variety of approaches have been developed for evaluating alternatives by comparing them with objectives, or with the strategies of competing forces. A basic problem in developing a decision-making technique, however, is information on the outcome of the alternatives and a ranking of the decision-makers alternatives. This means that the effectiveness of the device depends upon the effectiveness of methods to predict alternatives and to determine and evaluate the objectives of the decision maker. When the problem of matching competing strategies is considered it also means discovering and analyzing the objectives of competing systems.

As we consider the decision function, it becomes evident that the goals and objectives are critical factors in the evaluation of the alternatives and that information about them is as important as information about the system. Current research is pioneering in this area, and some of the terms associated with this work are "value theory" and "utility theory." The focus here is on the development of methods to quantify values so that they can enter into the decision function. Because of the importance of this aspect of the decision function, the study of value or utility is a field in itself. This problem is a favorite topic in books on decision making.

A dominant theme throughout the work to improve problem solving in the business firm is the application of knowledge and theory from the field of statistics to devise a mechanism for decision making, which deals not only with selecting alternatives but also with analysis that takes place prior to the decision making. Irwin D. J. Bross in his very readable book, *Design for Decision*,[20] seeks to introduce the reader to some ideas which seek to integrate predictions, values, and choice in the construction and operation of what he calls a "decision maker."

A Decision-Maker is considered to be a machine. Into the machine flows information; out of the machine comes a recommended course of action. The mechanism consists of three basic components. The Prediction System deals with alternative futures. The Value System handles the various conflicting purposes. The Criterion integrates the other two components and selects an appropriate action.[21]

APPLIED RESEARCH WITHIN A FIELD OR INDUSTRY

In addition to developing a generalized approach, there is, of course, no reason why applied research cannot also focus on the problem-solving process within a field of business administration or within an industry.

It could seek, for example, to develop a general approach that would seek to improve problem-solving capability within a field or industry. Business games have been constructed to simulate problem-solving situations peculiar to a field or industry. Possibilities would include business games for accountants, the petroleum industry, and so forth.

Research could develop methods of dealing with aspects of the problem-solving process that would be peculiar to a field or discipline. Instead of a generalized method for dealing with information, we could develop one peculiar to such areas as finance, marketing, and department stores. We could consider methods for analyzing the operating system, environment, and goals appropriate for an industry or field. Other possibilities would be specialized forecasting and decision-making techniques.

---

[20] Irwin D. J. Bross, *Design for Decision*, The Macmillan Co., New York, 1953.
[21] *Ibid.*, p. 32.

TABLE 3 Research to Improve Managerial Problem Solving

Develop Methods or Propose Solutions to Improve Managerial Problem Solving	Problem Analysis	Prediction	Decision Making
I. Methods and techniques which deal with entire process	Develop a method which focuses on all aspects of the problem-solving process—problem analysis, prediction, and decision making. Both business games and the case method do this by putting individual in position to go through all these aspects of process.		
II. Methods and techniques which deal with one or more aspects of process	Develop methods to secure information on system and environment, to analyze system and environment, to determine goals, to develop alternatives, to predict, or to make decisions.		
III. Prescribe solution to a general problem	Suggest an information-processing technique, an organization structure, an analysis of a customer's behavior, a set of goals for the business firm, a set of alternatives for some problem, the probable outcome of some business policy, and a decision for a specific set of circumstances.		
IV. Methods and techniques which deal with entire process in a field or industry	Develop a method which deals with all aspects of the problem-solving process within a field or industry. Building a business game for accountants or for the truck transportation industry, for example.		
V. Methods and techniques which deal with one or more aspects of process in a field or industry	Same as II but limited to problems of a field such as marketing or finance or to an industry such as food retailing, small metal manufacturing, and air transportation.		
VI. Prescribe solution to a general problem of a field or industry	Same as III but limited to problems of a field or industry.		
VII. Develop solution to a specific problem in a specific situation	Develop solution for a specific problem of a specific organization such as whether or not a given bank should automate its information processing, build a model of a manufacturing firm's inventory system, and so forth.		

Another possibility for problem-solving research would be studies to develop solutions or recommendations for problems considered to be general. Rather than recommend a technique or building models to analyze an inventory system, we could recommend a model or formula to be used in controlling inventory. Rather than recommend a method to use in building an administrative organization, we could recommend specific administrative structures. Other possibilities would be to prescribe accounting systems, forecast the demand for a specific product, or recommend a specific decision for an industry which is facing a series of alternatives and must select one of them.

Last, of course, is research dealing with the specific problems of specific situations. This type of research would be the application of methods developed by others to solve the specific problems of a company. Operations research has developed a variety of techniques to deal with the various aspects of the problem-solving process. The other phase of its work is the application of these techniques to specific situations. The results of this type of work are seldom published except, as a rule, in the form of case studies to illustrate the application of a method. Some of the results of this work may also be used to develop a case to be used in training procedures.

Table 3 seeks to depict the various possible alternatives of applied business research in contributing to improving the capability of business administration in the operation and management of business firms.

SCIENTIFIC METHOD AND APPLIED RESEARCH

Now although problem-solving research focuses its attention on the solution of operating problems and not on the development of knowledge to explain the nature of the world, it is critical that problem-solving research—if it is to be scientific—does not ignore concept formation, theories, laws, principles, assumptions, and hypotheses which are typically associated with basic research. To ignore them is to ignore the method and the product of scientific inquiry. They are as important to applied research as to basic research. Their role, perhaps, is different.

Theory, for example, can aid the applied researcher in several ways. It can provide the basis for making inferences about the phenomena which the applied researcher seeks to manipulate. Toulmin has suggested an analogy that might be helpful; a theory is like a map,[22] in that it indicates the nature of the terrain but does not provide an itinerary. From the map we could draw inferences, however, in making up an itinerary.

From economic theory we have the law or principle of diminishing returns:

As we hold a fixed input constant and increase a variable input, the marginal-physical-product of the variable input will decline—at least after a point.[23]

From this principle, the applied researcher dealing with production planning, let us say, can attempt to determine the marginal product and find that point at which it will decline. Economic theory also suggests that, at some point, as output increases, marginal cost will increase and marginal revenue will decrease. The inference to be drawn is the well-known one that profit will, therefore, be maximized where marginal cost and revenue are equal.

The work of professional psychologists has indicated the existence of the subconscious mind and its relationship to the behavior of people. From this theory marketing has drawn the inference that in influencing people's buying practices or in planning the sale of products, information should be gathered on the subconscious mind of the potential customers. Out of this has grown motivation research.

Theory, including principles and laws, does not provide information on the state of the world but only on the nature of the world. The applied researcher is, of course, primarily interested in the state of the world. Theory, however, will suggest to him how he can proceed to study the state of the world. Theory provides the applied researcher with a set of concepts and infor-

---

[22] Stephen Toulmin, *The Philosophy of Science,* Hutchinson's University Library, 1953, Ch. IV, "Theory and Maps," pp. 105–109.
[23] Paul A. Samuelson, *Economics, An Introductory Analysis,* McGraw-Hill Book Co., New York, 1955, p. 491.

mation on the relationship between or among the concepts. This information will serve to guide the applied researcher in the collection of data and in the interpretation of the data collected. A model of an organization or some part of the organization cannot be built without first having a set of concepts available. Theory can provide this information. The researcher using these can then collect data and proceed to construct his model. The determination of an organization's goals will be greatly helped by a theory which deals with the manner in which individuals or organizations form and use their goals. A theory of human creativity could certainly contribute to the development of a technique to improve the ability to develop alternative courses of action. Possibly we can best appreciate the role of theory in applied research by considering its possible contribution to forecasting. There can be two approaches to predicting. One approach uses and relies on theory, the other does not. The approach that does not rely on theory simply relies on the recognition of existing relationships for which theory is not yet adequate. For example, we can develop an effective method for predicting the phases of the moon by simply noting the number of sunsets between full moons. The technique would be accurate, but it would be prediction without understanding, without theory. There would be no understanding of the laws of astronomy. In a similar fashion, we can predict life expectancy, population growth, sales trends, and the behavior of customers by simply observing events and projecting trends. Two cities or companies could have similar rates of growth but for very different reasons. The weakness of this type of prediction is that if the prediction fails, it would not always be possible to determine why the failure took place.

The other approach, based on theory, is the more reliable because it is based on understanding. To use theory to predict phases of the moon would mean basing the prediction on a well-developed body of knowledge explaining the relationships between the moon, the earth, and the sun. To use theory to predict the results of specific courses of action would mean that each alternative would be considered in terms of the body of knowledge in which it falls. If the theory involved a financial decision, it would be necessary to determine if pertinent theory were available from which inferences could be made to predict the outcome. Since theory results from basic research, it becomes obvious that basic research can be critical to efficient predictions. The success of engineers has been made possible by the tremendous success in the physical sciences in the development of theory. Basic research in the newer social sciences, compared with that in the older physical sciences, has shown only moderate success; hence, theory has not been as helpful in prediction. This fact helps to explain the tendency for decision makers in the area of the social sciences to ignore theory or rely on weak or inapplicable theory.

In his attempt to solve problems, the applied researcher finds himself in the fortunate position of being able to draw upon theory from several fields. In developing methods to improve on the ability to market products, he can draw not only upon theory from economics but also psychology, social psychology, and statistics. Bierman, Fouraker, and Jaedicke in their book, *Quantitative Analysis for Business Decisions,* suggest an approach to solving the problem of determining the appropriate order size to replenish inventory based on ideas drawn from economic and statistical theory. Marginal analysis suggests that, as the size of the order is increased, a point will be reached where marginal gain will equal marginal loss. The order should not exceed this point, since with additional items ordered the marginal gain will be less than marginal profits. Probability theory suggests the idea of determining the probabilities of the marginal gain and marginal loss based on the probability of selling the items ordered. By combining these two ideas, the authors develop "expected marginal loss" and "expected marginal profit." [24]

Applied research based on theory is in strong contrast to problem-solving research based on nothing more than simple trial and error or uncritical imitation. This would be applied research at a simple or elementary level. The problem of inventory control can be approached in this way. We may try various ideas until we discover one that will function with a minimum of disruptions. This method may result in overordering and hence

---

[24] Harold Bierman, Lawrence E. Fouraker, and Robert K. Jaedicke, *Quantitative Analysis for Business Decisions,* Richard D. Irwin, Homewood, Ill., 1961, p. 61.

keep more funds invested in inventory than is justifiable, but this procedure may be used because it operates without disruptions and requires few periodic decisions. Another solution to the inventory problem would be to imitate a technique which appears to operate satisfactorily for some other organization. Again the results may produce a smooth, though inefficient, operation. Although it is also true that either of these approaches can result in an efficient inventory control system, if they are developed in an uncritical fashion, the approach to solving the problem cannot be considered scientific; it cannot be considered to be based on scientific method.

The role that theory can play in aiding applied research may seem obvious, but this role is too frequently ignored in applied research. The typical pattern in traditional applied business research is to seek to solve problems as though there were no pertinent theory available. Both engineering and medicine have demonstrated the importance of theory in their research and particularly theory from related disciplines.

This role which theory can play in problem solving underlines the importance and significance to business administration of the social sciences. These disciplines are primarily concerned with the development of theory to explain phenomena in their respective domain. They are, in Toulmin's analogy, map makers. Business administration is concerned with traveling, and obviously a map can provide a critical guide to traveling. For anyone to engage in applied research in business administration, it is incumbent upon him to learn the theory in pertinent disciplines in the social sciences. In fact, if he is at all serious about doing problem-solving research, it is difficult to comprehend how he could be very effective without a thorough understanding of what pertinent social scientists have learned. For example, if he were concerned with organizational administration, he could not do very much without a thorough understanding of organizatiton theory developed by such groups as the social psychologists and the cultural anthropologists. Too often applied research in administration begins with a set of convictions setting forth maxims for a sound organization.

Business administration is sometimes critical of the social sciences for not prescribing solutions to the problems of business.

However, this is asking the social scientist to draw inferences from his theories for business problem solving, and it is also assuming that he understands the objectives of business. The engineer does not expect the physicist to draw inferences and make recommendations for bridge construction. The responsibility for drawing inferences from the theory of the social scientists to lead to the solution of business problems rests with research in business administration.

Not infrequently, of course, the applied researcher finds it necessary to supplement theory with assumptions. The available theory may be too general to be pertinent to the specific situation with which he is dealing. Economic theory may be too general to be of value in seeking to evaluate alternative locations for a salt water aquarium. The researcher may, therefore, have to develop assumptions about the economics of salt-water aquarium operation and the behavior of potential customers. These assumptions, like theory, will be about the nature of the world.

In addition to theory and supplemental assumptions about the nature of the world, it may also be necessary to make assumptions about the state of the world. At least in the early development of a technique, it may be necessary to develop assumptions about the state of the world and then modify them as the technique is actually applied to a specific problem. To develop a method of evaluating proposed financial investments, we can draw upon economic and financial theory and then add assumptions about the nature of the world and the state of the world. Usually, two types of assumptions are made jointly in supplementing theory. As the empirical research precedes, both types of assumptions may be modified as we learn about the phenomena.

The role of assumptions is frequently emphasized in material dealing with the solutions to problems. In an article discussing the problem of allocating selling efforts among sales districts, J. A. Nordin adopted the following assumptions: [25]

Concretely the following assumptions will be made to bring into relief the problem of allocation of selling effort among districts:

---

[25] J. A. Nordin, "Spatial Allocation of Selling Expense," *Journal of Marketing*, Vol. VII, No. 3 (January, 1943), pp. 210–219. Reprinted from the *Journal of Marketing*, national quarterly publication of the American Marketing Association.

1. There is one product, sold in two districts.
2. The time during which the planner expects to be interested in the affairs of his business is to be thought of as divided into a number of periods. He is to plan for the first period, on the supposition that the sales of every subsequent period are independent of the sales within the period selected for analysis.
3. The analysis will be carried on as though the facts of the period just concluded were expected to continue unchanged. Although the planner will expect certain changes in the external conditions to which his efforts are subject, it will be convenient to use the past facts as a background. In many cases there will be no other important guide, and in any case anticipations can easily be substituted for the past facts as guides for action.
4. In order that the substitutions among selling plans may be isolated, assume that all adjustments are subject to the condition that they shall leave unchanged the total selling expense in the two districts taken together. Thus, the object of making adjustments is to maximize the total sales of the two districts taken together, while maintaining the constant total of selling expense.
5. The only form of selling expense is the salaries of salesmen. Salary per man is constant, and the salesmen are completely interchangeable. Moreover, whichever district a man works in, his personal efficiency is the same. That is, his response to each of a sufficiently wide range of stimuli is the same as that of each other salesman, and is independent of the selection of the district in which he works.
6. Although actually the determination of a price policy is a pressing problem, it is separable from the allocation of selling effort given the price. Therefore, let it be assumed that the price is known, and is the same for both the districts.
7. The problem of deciding the optimum selling expense for the given period will not be considered. It will be assumed in accordance with assumption (4) above that the sole task is that of increasing sales without increasing the total selling cost of the two districts. While such a movement seems desirable, consideration of the whole plan of operation might dictate an increase in selling expense in each of the districts.

Frequently, it may be necessary for a researcher to engage in studies to test his assumptions as well as statements from theory, if he feels that they may not apply in the situation which he is investigating. If this is the case the researcher, of course, will be doing research to test hypotheses. This is the same type of research usually associated only with basic research. The applied researcher often does this type of rsearch, but for a different reason than the basic researcher. The basic researcher will engage in this type of research because of his interest in determining the nature of the world, while the problem-solving researcher is seeking this information to help in the solution of an operational problem.

The applied researcher may also find the concepts of existing theory inadequate or inappropriate and proceed, therefore, to develop his own. He will then need to at least make assumptions about the relationships between or among these concepts and others he is using. Before long, he will find himself heavily committed to research on the nature of the world. The existing theory is limited. He must bring to a stop his work on problem solving to increase his understanding of his phenomena through developing concepts, assumptions, and even testing relationships. At this point applied and basic research are virtually the same.

Through the use of theory, supplemental assumptions, and any knowledge derived from actually testing hypotheses about the nature of the world, the researcher then has a body of knowledge which he can use as a guide in seeking to develop a specific technique to solve a problem. To go back to Toulmin's analogy of the map, the researcher now has a map of his terrain, some of which may not have been empirically tested. With this map he can then proceed to try to develop an itinerary for a trip or propose a formula which can be used in preparing itineraries.

Given the theoretical framework, the researcher may then proceed to collect empirical data to indicate the state of the world. Or, put somewhat differently, given the nature of the world, we can then proceed to determine the state of the world. At this point, the researcher can bring into play data-gathering techniques for studying his phenomena. Theory and assumptions have indicated the concepts to be studied and why the concepts should be studied. After the data are collected, the researcher is then in a position to analyze them and propose a solution. The analysis will, like the fact gathering, be based on the theory. The proposed solution will be determined from the analysis.

The proposed solution which is developed can itself be treated as a hypothesis and subjected to test. A procedure for pricing, for inventory ordering, or for promotion might be examined to see if it accomplishes the desired results. The emphasis of the test will not be concerned with whether or not the formula explains phenomena, but rather with whether or not it provides satisfactory solutions to them.

4

Modern Business Research
and Basic Research

Even though business administration is an applied art, there is really no reason why it should not engage in basic research and there are many reasons why it should. The purpose of basic research is to develop theory, concepts, and principles which are critical both to explaining phenomena and to problem solving. Basic disciplines such as economics and sociology develop theoretical knowledge which proves very helpful to problem solving in business administration; but basic research in business is in a better position to focus its attention on the phenomena that may be of most significance to business problem solving. Business research conducted within a university setting also has an obligation, as do other academic areas, simply to increase human understanding irrespective of any specific operational problem that may be facing the business community.

Many have been critical of business research in the university, feeling that it has ignored this last responsibility and overemphasized applied research. We feel, however, that traditional business research in the university has not devoted enough attention to both basic and applied research and has overemphasized fact gathering on the assumption that if enough facts are gathered together they will reveal the knowledge needed to understand phenomena and solve problems. Simply increasing the number or variety of empirical observations does not insure increasing understanding of phenomena and can, on the other hand, interfere with efforts to do so.

COMPONENTS OF BASIC RESEARCH

Under the label, "basic research," we find a wide range of activities. Roy Francis, in his book *The Rhetoric of Science*,[1] used three terms that can be helpful to classify the various aspects of scientific investigation: *inquiry* (qualitative research), the investigation to develop concepts, principles, hypotheses, and theories; *research* (quantitative research), empirically testing the ideas developed in qualitative research; and *analysis,* the interpretation of facts through the use of theory. Analysis which might be more appropriately labeled "interpretation" does not investigate theory but, rather, relies on theory to guide in the collection and the interpretation of data. This activity is appropriately an aspect of applied research and can provide the basis for the solution of operational problems.

Robert Brown in *Explanation in Social Science* [2] discussed three aspects of investigation by students of social behavior: reporting, description, and explanation. "Reporting" gives a direct account of events without indicating why or how they occurred. Description goes beyond this and gives an explanation of the events reported.

Now compare this with what is usually called "reporting." For there are a number of differences between pure reporting and pure describing, even though there are intermediate forms in which they are blended. Merely to report something is to give an account of it or to tell someone what occurred, and it may be that no description will be employed in the telling. "A small kangaroo and a man walking home from his office collided last evening in Canberra" is not a description, if by "description" we have in mind only the mentioning of characteristic features. The sentence taken by itself is a report. On the other hand, to describe something is to tell someone what some state of affairs is like. A successful description enables its auditor to recognize what has been described to him, when he will not otherwise be able to do so. A

---

[1] Roy G. Francis, *The Rhetoric of Science,* University of Minnesota Press, Minneapolis, Minn., 1961.
[2] Robert Brown, *Explanation in Social Science,* Aldine Publishing Co., Chicago. Copyright 1963 by Robert Brown.

successful report need not do this; though it may if it includes a description.[3]

Brown felt the distinction between "reporting" and "describing" to be a legitimate one and used it to contradict critics, particularly physical scientists, who contend that students of social behavior engage in "mere descriptions." Brown felt that description provides valuable insight to increasing understanding of phenomena. He, however, goes on to say that explanation distinguishes the social observer from the social scientist. "If what we have said is correct, social observers are typically interested in establishing statements about particular events and the operation of particular causes. On the other hand, social scientists properly attempt to do more than this; they try to establish sound generalizations about classes of events." [4]

Francis and Brown's classifications are not inconsistent with each other and together suggest a possible conceptual scheme for regarding basic research in business administration—with the exception of Francis' concept, "analysis" which is more closely associated with applied research. With some variations in the use of the terms by these two authors, the concepts will be combined to provide a framework for the discussion here of the various aspects of basic research. The discussion will first consider reporting and description, neither of which accomplishes scientific explanation but may contribute to it. Explanation depends upon the development of generalizations and their verification. Next will be a review of inquiry or qualitative research—which is a most creative aspect of basic research, inasmuch as it develops new concepts, principles, hypotheses, and theories. Last is a discussion of quantitative research which empirically tests relationships developed in inquiry.

REPORTING—FACT GATHERING

Brown's concept "reporting" can be broken down into two additional concepts—reporting based on well-developed concepts drawn from theory and reporting based on rather general con-

---

[3] *Ibid.,* pp. 15–16.
[4] *Ibid.,* p. 40.

cepts. The latter would be research, at a primitive level at best, simple fact gathering. The concepts used are loosely related, if at all, and may have been borrowed from conversational language. An example of this approach would be a report on a community's manufacturing establishments, giving detailed statistics on manufacturing classified by size, industry, and location. These are rather general concepts without any special theoretical basis. This type of report is similar to a census report or a statistical abstract.

Another example of such reporting would be an account of business practices in pricing merchandise. An account which did not explain the practices or answer the questions of "why" and "how"—but simply "what"—would be limited to a factual report of practices. Other examples of this type of work would include surveys of banking practices, accounting conventions, and customer purchases.

Simple reporting, though not very sophisticated, is not necessarily easy or inexpensive to do. A good survey can be challenging and expensive. The question, however, is whether or not it should be done or at least whether or not it should be labeled "research." This type of work can be very useful but should not normally be brought under the guise of basic research. It is simple fact gathering and nothing more.

As an aspect of research, simple reporting is seldom justified. It might be appropriate when a new discipline is being developed which has virtually no theoretical concepts, or where a new area in an existing discipline is being explored and needs to be surveyed to provide general information about the phenomena. If nothing is known theoretically or otherwise about retailing or industrial wage structures, a meaningful point of departure could well be to observe and classify our observations using rather general concepts. The important prerequisite would be no theoretical information. A significant innovation in an activity otherwise well understood might suggest a report as a start toward basic research. Research on an innovation such as the discount house could begin with reporting. As a general rule, however, where possible, research should seek to begin at a point beyond just collection and classification. Only under very special circumstances should basic research legitimately begin with simple reporting using general concepts. Most fact-gathering studies based on general concepts cannot be justified as a point of departure to provide material for discovering and studying relationships and contributing to theory. Man's knowledge is far too advanced in most fields and disciplines to justify this approach for basic research.

Reports based on theoretical concepts operate at a more sophisticated level. If we have a reliable theory indicating the relationships between production, average costs, marginal costs, average revenues, and marginal revenues, we could use these concepts as a basis for reporting on business firms. If we were interested in a report on the retail industry in Atlanta, Georgia, such an approach would suggest that the report be based on concepts drawn from a theory of retailing, economics, or human behavior. An example of this type of fact gathering in economics would be some of the data prepared by the Council of Economic Advisors for the Joint Economics Committee. In their monthly report, *Economic Indicators*,[5] they include in a chart: data on Gross National Product, Personal Consumption Expenditures, Government Purchases of Goods and Services, Gross Private Domestic Investment, and Net Export of Goods and Services. These concepts have a theoretical basis, and the report is considerably more sophisticated and valuable than one that would be based on rather general concepts, unrelated theoretically. Frequently, people think that they are doing this type of reporting when they are, in reality, doing the type of simple fact gathering previously discussed. They have deluded themselves into assuming their concepts have theoretical import. They have failed, however, to critically and explicitly examine their concepts prior to use. This type of reporting is justified only where there is virtually no theoretical knowledge. Reporting based on sound theoretical concepts should be the more typical type if a study must be limited to fact gathering.

Obviously, it would be quite difficult to satisfactorily classify all data gathering reports into either of the two categories, and this is not what is proposed. The suggestion is that any fact

---

[5] Council of Economic Advisors, *Economic Indicators*, United States Printing Office, Washington, D.C.

gathering which is designed to contribute to basic research should, where possible, be based on theoretically related concepts rather than general concepts. However, this may not always be possible, so that fact gathering based on general concepts can be justified when nothing else is available. But every effort should be made to move toward fact gathering based on theoretically related concepts which will help to assure meaningful data collection.

Whether reporting is based on concepts drawn from theory or on something less sophisticated, such as conversational language, it should not alone be considered research, basic or any other kind, but an aspect of research. It can be of value in contributing to the development of concepts, principles, and theories and in testing hypotheses. Generally, there are much better strategies that can be followed. Reporting and fact gathering can be a most sterile activity in doing basic research.

DESCRIPTION

Closer to basic research would be a study which not only reports data but seeks to study patterns, regularities, and relationships. If well done, it will provide an integrated statement to explain specific empirical events. In reporting on a business practice, description would not only indicate the practice but also seek to explain the specific business practice. Description incorporates reporting with analysis of the material reported. Description, like reporting, can be based on concepts drawn from theory or from conversational language.

If based on nontheoretical concepts, analysis in description will tend to be something of a trial and error activity. It will involve sifting through the data and attempting to spot significant patterns. The analysis will be elementary. On the other hand, if we use concepts suggested by theory, the study will tend to be more valuable. The theory will suggest concepts to use in collecting data and will suggest concepts which should be related to each other.

Illustrative of the approach using nontheoretical concepts would be to take the latest census of the United States population and pore over it looking for significant patterns. We could do the same thing with the *Statistical Abstract of the United States, Sale's Management's Survey of Power,* and *Fortune's* annual survey of the five hundred largest corporations. Another possibility would be to collect data on wholesaling practices in the Southwest and then see what significant patterns we could find revealed. Another possibility would be to collect cost data on filling stations' operation and analyze it. Often, the most that such studies produce is a report with limited analysis rather than a meaningful description.

Where possible, the investigator should begin with a theory. Before gathering data on wholesaling in the Southwest, the researcher should first set forth his theory which will provide his argument for the data to be collected. The data collection will then be based on the best theoretical information available. The study may then proceed to analyze patterns, regularities, and relationships.

Where there is no theory, the investigator would do well to set forth a series of assumptions about his phenomena as the basis for his description. This would, in effect, be setting up a theory to guide his work. There can be virtually no justification for description based on nontheoretical concepts drawn from conversational language. To follow this approach is too elementary. As in reporting, description based on nontheoretical concepts is difficult to justify. Man's knowledge is so well advanced that there is virtually no area for which a theory is not pertinent or where he cannot develop a series of assumptions to guide his research.

A very good example of description is the study *Accounting in Small Business Decisions* [6] by James L. Gibson and W. Warren Haynes, in which the practices of approximately one hundred small business firms were analyzed. The study reports on the procedures used and then seeks to indicate why the firms used them. The study, however, does not seek to generalize. The study also has some aspect of applied research, in that it suggests alternative procedures that firms should consider using.

---

[6] James L. Gibson and W. Warren Haynes, *Accounting in Small Business Decisions,* University of Kentucky Press, Lexington, Ky. 1963.

Two additional examples of description would be *The First Two Years: Problems of Small Firm Growth and Survival*[7] and *A Pilot Study of Successful and Unsuccessful Small Business Enterprises Within Montana.*[8] In the first example eighty-one firms were studied over a two-year period following their opening. The focus of the study was on the factors affecting the firms ability to survive during the first two years of their operation. The study reported on these factors and sought to analyze them as well. The second study, using an hypothesis as a guide, interviewed a number of firms in Montana. The study also reported its findings and analyzed them to discover patterns and regularities. This study did not generalize, even though it used an hypothesis to guide its data collection and analysis.

The serious limitation of descriptive studies is their failure to generalize from their observations, which is the basis of scientific explanation—the work of developing and testing principles, laws, and theories. Description, where it uses hypotheses and indicates the form of regularities, deals with the state of the world and is highly empirical. This is not the same as building a systematic explanation for phenomena. A series of descriptive studies of wholesaling in the fifty states can be very well done. Relationships, patterns, and regularities can be carefully analyzed, but the studies will not provide scientific explanation unless generalizations are drawn from the analysis. Generalization leaps from descriptive material to a conclusion that a law-like relationship has been found. Description might make a study of six firms to indicate the relationship between cost and production. Generalization would conclude that the six studies provide sufficient information to generalize about the relationship.

The physical scientist is primarily concerned with the development of generalizations. When he criticizes the students of social behavior as developing mere descriptions, he is emphasizing their

---

[7] Kurt B. Mayer and Sidney Goldstein, *The First Two Years: Problems of Small Firm Growth and Survival,* Small Business Administration, Washington, D.C., 1961.

[8] Edward J. Chambers and Raymond L. Gold, *A Pilot Study of Successful and Unsuccessful Small Business Enterprises Within Montana,* Bureau of Business and Economic Research, Montana State University, Missoula, Mont., 1963.

failure to generalize and admittedly, the social scientist has often had to satisfy himself with descriptive research. The social scientist has not been as successful as the physical scientist in controlling variables, reducing the number of variables to be analyzed, developing measures, and theorizing. These formidable problems have, unfortunately, tended not only to limit social science research to description but also to overemphasize reporting. Description can be considered to be basic research. It does increase understanding. It does explain but does not develop theory, the basic goal of basic research. Description can help invent new concepts, and its work can certainly help in the development of theory.

INQUIRY—QUALITATIVE RESEARCH

The basic objective of scientific explanation is the development of concepts, laws, principles, hypotheses, and theories. This is the work which Francis called "inquiry" or "qualitative" research. Here it is given a broader meaning than Francis gives it. He associates it primarily with developing hypotheses. Both reporting and description can contribute to inquiry. They provide empirical material that can stimulate efforts to develop adequate concepts, suggest hypotheses about concepts, or analyze principles.

Inquiry is a very creative and exciting aspect of basic research. It is similar to the creative work of the artist, the composer, the author, the sculptor. To do it well, however, requires that the investigator be thoroughly familiar with existing theory and its implications. Like the artist or composer, he must know his subject well and understand the contributions of his predecessors and contemporaries.

The varied manifestations of creativity, be they ingenious and revolutionary ideas or artistic masterpieces, are not generated spontaneously and without an appropriate background. Suggestions for stimulating creativity may be found by studying the training, methods, and accomplishments of great men. The popular conception that Newton, on being struck by a falling apple, spontaneously discovered the law of gravitation is incorrect. Newton had accumulated a vast store of knowledge in one of the finest institutions of learning of his time, and he had received profound and detailed scientific training. His discoveries were a consequence of much thought and experimentation, and his knowledge of Kepler's results provided a basis for the discovery of the law of gravitation. Simply stated, a creative individual is also most likely to be a trained individual. Training provides exposure to creative ideas as well as the facts and discipline which permit concrete results from creative activity.[9]

This aspect of basic research often deceives the would-be investigator. No doubt the challenge is intriguing, but the prospects of being successful in this area are limited unless the individual is well trained in his field and understands well the principles of scientific investigation. It also takes a highly creative person to make significant contributions in this area. Part of the lure of doing this type of research is the fact that one can do it from his desk without the annoyances, inconveniences, and the expense of empirical investigation: it is abstract and can be much "neater" than the empirical problems of securing data to test theoretical ideas; it has been referred to as "clean" research while empirical research has been referred to as "dirty work." There are also status symbols involved—the novice and the graduate student are to do the empirical research, while the senior man does the theoretical work.

For most investigators the potential for successful research in inventing concepts and principles and developing new theory is challenging. This is not so much a comment on human ability as it is on the fact that significant breakthroughs in science occur on the extreme frontiers of knowledge and are infrequent. This is not to say that the individual should necessarily be discouraged from doing basic research in this area, but rather that it would be advisable, if he seeks to invest his time and energies in research in this area, for him to be well aware of what he seeks to do and the potentialities of his success. Testing hypotheses drawn from existing theory can provide a very fruitful field for basic research. It is as important as the other aspect of basic research and needs to be done to test ideas developed in inquiry.

Cyert and March in their book, *A Behavioral Theory of the*

---

[9] From Thomas L. Saaty, *Mathematical Methods of Operations Research*, McGraw-Hill Book Co., New York, 1959, pp. 383–384. Used by permission.

Firm, seek to make a contribution which results from what we have been calling inquiry. They discuss existing concepts and theories of the firm and then proceed to set forth new concepts and a new theory.

The basic framework for analysis we have proposed, like the classic one, has two major organizing devices: (1) It has a set of exhaustive variable categories; (2) It has a set of relational concepts.[10]

They argue that they can analyze decision making in the modern firm in terms of variables affecting organization goals, expectations, and choice. Their major relational concepts are the following four: quasi resolution of conflict, problemistic search, uncertainty avoidance, and organizational learning.

QUANTITATIVE RESEARCH—EMPIRICAL TESTING

Roy Francis in his concept "research" (also labeled quantitative research) was suggesting investigation designed to test empirically hypotheses drawn from theory, ideas developed in inquiry. The objective of this approach is to develop techniques to identify concepts and relationships and thus collect data, test hypotheses, and develop evidence to support generalizations. The hypotheses may be drawn from theory which may be well established or which may consist, to a great extent, of reasonable assumptions and logical but untested conclusions. The feasibility of this approach depends, of course, upon the existence of some knowledge or assumptions about phenomena. Since there is theory pertinent to most phenomena, it can be assumed that as a rule this approach can usually be taken in almost any field or discipline.

This approach is considerably different from reporting and description. The difference from reporting is probably obvious. It differs from description, because the focus is on testing an hypothesis and seeking to generalize the finding. An hypothesis can guide description, but the results would be limited to the empirical study rather than generalization.

---

[10] Richard M. Cyert and James G. March, *A Behavioral Theory of the Firm,* Prentice-Hall, Englewood Cliffs, New Jersey, 1963, p. 115.

This type of research uses hypotheses suggested by theory and not by data. If we are just studying masses of data, we can find relationships which may be spurious and not significant at all. The study of population data might suggest that the children per family tends to be higher among those families living near the railroad tracks than elsewhere. It would be somewhat difficult to generalize that the proximity of the tracks and trains has a direct relationship to the number of children born. Theory might suggest a more meaningful way to think about the phenomena, possibly in terms of education, income, and land values.

By beginning with hypotheses as the basis for the study and the collection of data, the investigator carefully plans his data collecting to study relationships which existing knowledge suggests are reasonable topics to investigate. This helps to eliminate the collection of useless data and to emphasize planning the collection of the data. The investigator will have a firmer control over what he is doing and a better understanding of the meaning of the data which he is getting.

If empirical research takes as its point of departure, theory and hypotheses drawn from the theory, it will be using as firm a foundation as is available for the work. This approach will provide an orientation for the data collection and reduce random or casual searching. Beginning with the theory will, of necessity, cause the investigator to study theory carefully. This will acquaint him with available knowledge and either provide a model or provide the basis for building his model to guide him in his research.

Theory can suggest a number of research alternatives to the empirical investigator. He can, for example, question the axioms, assumptions, or premises of the theory. If these are stated in terms of relationships between concepts, he will have hypotheses to use as his point of departure. He could take from economic theory the principle of decreasing cost or diminishing returns and consider the principle to be an hypothesis. He can then use it as a guide to collect data. On the other hand, he could take one of the conclusions given by theory and use it as an hypothesis to test. A very interesting possibility for basic research is to investigate the problem of measuring and identifying concepts drawn from theory. This is particularly challenging in the case of constructs where one must find manifestations to measure since the construct cannot be measured directly.

One of the most challenging opportunities for research is to combine inquiry and empirical research in the overall evaluation of theory as a satisfactory explanation for phenomena. This involves consideration of the basic principles of the theory, in addition to the axioms and theorems and evaluation of the logic and extent to which the theorems can validly be drawn from the premises.

The challenge to creativity in empirical research is the successful development of devices to measure concepts and to identify relationships. This challenge to creativity is as great, probably, as the creative challenge in inquiry. Possibly, in empirical research we might find the word ingenuity more appropriate. Effective empirical research certainly requires ingenuity. Concepts are inventions of the human mind and are not products or creatures of man's environment. The empirical investigator, therefore, is faced with the task of attempting to fit the concepts to the environment or vice versa. If he is interested in the construct, authority, he must find some way to identify specific aspects of the environment as authority. Once the concepts have been satisfactorily identified, the next step is the development of a method for examining the relationships set forth in the theory.

An interesting device currently being used to study the relationships of theory and which shows considerable promise is the construction of computer models. Cyert and March in their book, *A Behavioral Theory of the Firm*,[11] included a discussion of several computer models which were built based on the theory they set forth in the book. Their approach was to simulate on the computer, operating procedures of the specific phenomena, such as the pricing rules of a department store or one of its departments. Output from the simulation is then compared with output from the phenomena where both have a similar input. Balderston and Hoggatt, in *Simulation of Market Processes*,[12] prepared a simulation of the market behavior of the lumber industry on the

---

[11] *Ibid.*

[12] Frederick E. Balderston and Austin C. Hoggatt, *Simulation of Market Processes*, Institute of Business and Economic Research, Berkeley, Calif., 1962.

west coast and then used the simulation to test a series of hypotheses drawn from theory.

A more traditional approach is illustrated by the doctoral dissertation *The Effect of Capital Structure on the Cost of Capital* [13] by Alexander Barges. In this study he undertook "to test the validity of the hypothesis that the cost of capital to the firm is unaffected by capital structure formulated by Professor Franco Modigliani and Merton H. Miller in an article which has created controversy among both theorist and empiricist." In his research Barges used statistical methods to identify concepts and test relationships.

Although reporting, description, inquiry, and empirical testing have been discussed as separate categories, this does not mean they need to be done separately. Frequently, they are performed together in a single study. A descriptive study could provide material for the development of hypotheses to be tested empirically. A descriptive study could be preceded by inquiry which suggested hypotheses to be followed in conducting a descriptive study of some phenomena. Inquiry could also precede the preparation of a report.

It is also worth emphasizing again that the purpose of basic research is to provide an explanation for phenomena and not to solve operational problems. This means that the work of basic research and the language used is not in terms of solving operational problems, but in terms of providing an explanation to increase understanding of the nature of the phenomena involved. It talks about concepts and how they are related to each other, and not how they are supposed to be related. It seeks to provide a conceptual scheme for thinking about phenomena. It is important to keep this goal or purpose in mind when evaluating the results of basic research and when seeking to engage in basic research. Failure to understand this objective is responsible for the dissatisfaction and disillusionment with the results of basic research by many who are primarily concerned with solving operational problems, that is, people who have a "practical" orientation.

---

[13] Alexander Barges, *The Effect of Capital Structure on the Cost of Capital*, Prentice-Hall, Englewood Cliffs, N.J., 1963, p. 100.

BASIC RESEARCH IN BUSINESS ADMINISTRATION

If it is accepted that business administration in an institution of higher education has a responsibility for basic research, then the fields of business—such as accounting, marketing, finance, and management—should engage in projects to undertake the various aspects of research that were just discussed. The studies could be limited to reporting and description where appropriate, or they could attempt to develop new concepts, principles, and theories and develop techniques to test these ideas empirically. The goal of basic research in business—as anywhere—would, of course, be to increase understanding of phenomena. Basic research in marketing would seek to increase understanding of phenomena falling within its purview. It would not be research to increase the ability of the firm to market products and services.

An example of basic research in marketing would be a study of advertising and social values. The results of such research might indicate that advertising tends to alter social values over a period of time and suggest the way it does this. There would be no comment on how to improve advertising. Another possibility would be to study the relationship between advertising and customer decisions to buy. A somewhat less utilitarian study would be one to determine the factors affecting the techniques and strategies of the advertising industry.

Examples of basic research in the other disciplines of business administration could be given: A study in management could be made to determine the factors affecting the employee's image of the company and management's image of the employee. Another study could be the background of executives. An example in finance would be a study of the cost functions of installment loans or the sociological factors affecting the judgment of the bank's lending activities. An interesting study in accounting might be the behavior of department heads under various budgeting and overhead allocation methods; another accounting study would be the development of cost and revenue curves. On a broad basis would be a general study of business administration, such as the relationship between business and political leaders.

As we consider various examples of basic research in the numerous fields of business administration, we note the frequency with which such studies also tend to fall into an area where social scientists are engaged in research. It may mean that a student of business administration who emphasizes basic research becomes a social scientist who has singled out an area called business for the subject of his basic research. An accountant, for example, when he becomes involved in studying cost and revenue curves, is doing the sort of thing that an economist is doing. He is a behavioral scientist when he studies the behavior of people under varying methods of setting budgets and allocating overhead.

If the various fields of business administration were to increase their emphasis on basic research, there would be the possibility that, in time, they would become sciences rather than applied arts. Conceptually, at least, marketing could become a social science whose purview or domain were that aspect of society which involved marketing behavior. Such a result, however, could lead to a reduction or elimination of marketing's focus on the solution of operational problems of people involved in marketing. The same thing could happen in engineering. As electrical engineering increased its emphasis on basic research, it would reduce the emphasis on the solution of operational problems, and it might become a little difficult to distinguish electrical engineering from physics. As marketing became more of a social science, it might be difficult to distinguish it from either sociology or psychology.

Presumably, the fields of business administration have as one of their major responsibilities research on the operational problems of the business firm. As long as this responsibility continues, research should have as one of its principle goals the solution of operational problems of the business firm. This does not mean that business administration should not engage in basic research, but rather that it should consider the integration of basic research and applied research. This implies that business research should be closely integrated with the work of the social sciences. Business administration really has the dual responsibility of doing both basic and applied research.

Research in industry tends to be oriented almost exclusively to applied research, but even here some type of basic research might

be appropriate. Quinn and Cavanaugh in an article, "Fundamental Research Can be Planned," suggest a possible orientation
for basic research which could be applicable to both industry and
university. They distinguish between the aspects of basic research
—pure and fundamental. They think of pure research as investigation for the sake of increasing knowledge, while fundamental
research seeks knowledge with the objective of developing information which will lead to the solution of operational problems.

Fundamental research is not—like so-called "pure" research—the pursuit
of knowledge for its own sake. Fundamental research seeks knowledge
which will hopefully benefit someone someday. But the specific nature
of its eventual application is not known at the time the research is
performed. A company supports such research in the hope that it can
eventually exploit some percentage of new discoveries in the fields
under study.[14]

Their distinction may be a thin one, but they proceed in their
article to outline the idea that industry should do fundamental
research and follow the strategy of studying those topics or those
areas in which knowledge that will prove useful to them will
most probably develop. In the article Quinn and Cavanaugh are
primarily interested in research for product development. This
approach, however, could indicate a strategy for research in any
applied field, that is basic research on subjects that will probably
be most appropriate to operational problems pertinent to the
field. Basic research in marketing would emphasize areas pertinent to the operational problems of marketing, and this would
be true in accounting, finance, management, and other areas in
business administration.

---

[14] James Brian Quinn and Robert M. Cavanaugh, "Fundamental Research
Can be Planned," *Harvard Business Review*, Vol. 42, No. 1, p. 112.

5

Planning Research:
The Research Design

The arguments for planning a research project are probably not significantly different from the arguments for any other kind of planning. In the rational commitment of resources we seek to maximize the benefits from the commitment, and planning is a means for achieving this goal. In committing twenty-five thousand dollars for the construction of a house, prudence suggests the careful preparation of a floor plan and a set of specifications. If we were going to build a five million dollar bridge, a set of engineering plans are called for and much more planning than is needed for the twenty-five-thousand-dollar expenditure.

Planning prepares for the allocation of resources based on available knowledge. The architect, in drawing plans for a house, calls upon many sources of knowledge—information on building materials, functions of various parts of a house, on human living needs, local building codes, lending agencies specifications, and numerous other factors. It helps to insure the most efficient use of resources to build a house by relying on available knowledge, and the more knowledge that the architect has and can use, the more satisfactory will be the plans. Similarly, planning a research project seeks to use available knowledge to conduct the project.

In addition to calling upon available knowledge to guide resource use, planning also analyzes the problem to be solved by the resource commitment. A plan for the construction of a bridge should be based on analysis of the problem to be solved by the bridge's construction. Planning for a company's reorganization should be based on a careful determination of the problem to be solved.

Finally, planning specifies the approach which is to be used in the project. It indicates the strategy and the techniques to be followed. The specification may be general or very detailed. A plan for the investigation to develop a special advertising technique could limit itself to a general proposal, or it could set forth in great detail the steps to be followed in conducting the analysis.

A well-developed research design, like any plan, can provide a device not only to focus the work of the investigator but also provide a means of communicating to others the logic and reasoning for the project that is to be conducted. If a number of people are involved in the study the research design can serve as a document to summarize the thinking of the group. If approval for the project is being sought or if funds are being requested, the research design provides the arguments for the study.

Frequently, in implementing a plan, alterations will be made in the original proposal. This, however, does not negate the need to plan, since the purpose in planning is to undertake a task relying on as much pertinent information and analysis as is feasible or practical. To do otherwise is simply to ignore knowledge and rational consideration.

The aspects or components of preparing a research plan, more appropriately a research design, are: the topic, purpose, problem analysis, research strategy, research techniques, format for reporting results of study (report, article, book, problem-solving technique, recommendation, etc.), budget, and time schedule.

TOPIC

The topic or subject of a research project is certainly no statement of the problem to be solved by the study, although it is frequently thought to be. This is true notwithstanding how general or how specific the topic. General topics, such as the efficient introduction of data-processing equipment, the comparison of two theories, the applicability of linear programming to the solution of location problems, or the analysis of New York Stock Exchange regulations, do not indicate the problem to be solved by a proposed research project. Even very specific topics, however, should not be confused with the problem. For example, a research project's topic could be to test the hypothesis that the consumption of soft drinks in Amarillo, Texas, increases proportionately with increases in temperature. As specific as this is, it does not indicate the problem of the project which could turn out to include modifying a theory, developing a definition and a measure for both "consumption," and "temperature," designing an experiment, setting up a consumers panel, collecting sales and temperature records, and determining the form of the regularity. A study to determine an organization's goals may seem sufficiently straightforward, but the problem to be solved by the research is not known until the investigator has analyzed and formulated the problem. The topic or subject of a study indicates little more than a point of departure.

PURPOSE

Before analyzing his problem, the researcher needs to consider carefully the purpose or purposes to be served by the research, for they will provide him with some guide lines not only for the formulation of his problem but also for the overall research design. The purpose of a project provides the argument for even developing the design. If a particular problem is causing periodic breakdowns in an assembly-line operation and costing considerable amounts of money, the purpose would be to correct this difficulty and the value of solution would be measured in the money saved. If the purpose is to test several hypotheses suggested by a theory, the value of the research would be in terms of its implications for the theory and understanding of the phenomena involved.

In evaluating the purpose of the study the researcher will seek information which will provide a guide for the allocation of resources (including time) not only to the study but also to the development of the research design itself. A research design for a graduate student's paper, which is primarily a training device, would not require the time and effort that we would expect of a research design to study an industry-wide problem costing thousands of dollars or a study of basic theoretical questions underlying the foundations of a discipline's growth and development. Neither would one expect them to absorb the same resources in the study itself.

For the audience of the research design, a statement of purpose not only presents the argument for doing the project but provides the reader with an amplification of the topic or subject which has been chosen. Stating the purpose sets the stage and probably the tone of the research design.

The following are three illustrations of topics and purposes of the investigation.

Management According to Task: Organizational Differentiation

The purpose of this paper is to examine this vague and implicit belief in some general principles of uniform good practice; and to consider as an alternative the idea of "differentiation" in organizations, wherein good practice becomes largely a function of the task which each subpart of a complex organization is intended to perform.[1]

Food Distribution Center Location: Technique and Procedure

The specific task is to evaluate alternative techniques and measures for selecting market area locations for food distribution centers. In the supermarket industry, three geographic market configurations stand out as representative of normal spatial relationship among supermarkets. In two of these geographic retail market areas, considerable variation in distribution expense may result in accordance with distribution center locations. For research purposes, location models representing these two geographic retail market areas are simulated. By using models, alternative locations can be selected and tested under simulated conditions.[2]

The Supermarket: An Analysis of Growth, Development, and Change

As the title of this study suggests, the primary objectives are (1) identifying, (2) describing, and (3) analyzing the major forces that have lead to the post-World War II development, growth, and change of retail food supermarkets.[3]

---

[1] Harold J. Leavitt, "Management According to Task: Organizational Differentiation," *Management International*, January–February, 1962, p. 13.
[2] Donald J. Bowersox, *Food Distribution Center Location: Technique and Procedure*, Bureau of Business and Economic Research, Michigan State University, 1962, p. 7.
[3] Rom J. Markin, *The Supermarket: An Analysis of Growth Development and*

Typically, the author will go into more detail than these quotations might indicate. The author, in outlining his purpose, should go into detail to explain how the study may contribute to existing theory or to the development of a new technique for solving a problem. In fact, in the three references cited, the authors actually said more about the purpose than the material quoted. They wove it into their general discussion of the problem.

An ever-present problem for the would-be researcher is the source of worthwhile topics for investigation. This is not a significant problem for the applied researcher in the business firm, because the operation of the firm will generate material. Basic research in industry and both applied and basic research in the academic atmosphere, however, place the researcher in the position of deciding from many alternatives what is worth investigating. It is a good example of both the frustration and responsibility of free choice that come with any kind of freedom.

Probably no greater admonition can be given to the potential researcher, whether he is interested in applied or basic research, than to know his field well. The frustration of many a graduate student, and for that matter faculty members, in attempting to find a good research topic is often due to their limited knowledge of the field in which they wish to do research. Conversely, looking for a research topic can be very helpful in acquainting an individual with a field.

The serious researcher needs to keep abreast of developments in his field and closely related fields in order to be in a position to find topics and to meaningfully evaluate them. People both in industry and the university find it valuable to develop a system that will bring to their attention pertinent developments in their field in research interests.

PROBLEM ANALYSIS—BASIC RESEARCH

Research frequently fails to accomplish its purpose, because the investigator simply failed to understand adequately the problem to be solved. He may have found himself developing excellent

---

Change, Economic and Business Studies No. 36, Bureau of Business and Economic Research, Washington State University, January, 1963, p. 2.

answers for the wrong questions. Ackoff, in *The Design of Social Research*,[4] aptly made this point when he said, "It is an old and wise saying that 'a problem well put is half solved'."

Typically, the temptation is to assume the problem to be investigated and quickly move on to data gathering. As a result, the problem may be formulated very superficially, and hence the questions asked tend to be superficial and possibly irrelevant. Inadequate problem formulation has probably been one of the weakest aspects of traditional business research. Fact-gathering techniques have been the strong suit.

Review of Existing Knowledge. The frequent admonition to the investigator to "search the literature" is based on the assumption that a basic building block in problem analysis is the existing knowledge pertinent to the topic. This would include established theory and empirical evidence, plus speculations by experts and (in the case of applied research) techniques that have been developed.

The review of existing knowledge will tend to vary somewhat between basic and applied research. Since the basic researcher seeks to expand upon current knowledge to explain the nature of the phenomena, he is interested in the problems of unsatisfactory explanations, untested or inadequately tested hypotheses, re-examination of the inferences drawn from empirical data, poorly developed concepts, and conflicting theories.

Problem analysis in basic research will, therefore, review existing theoretical information that has been developed. If we were interested in the behavior of executives in medium size companies, we would review theoretical work which had been done in the area of organization behavior. This review could include reading existing literature and discussion with other specialists doing research on the topic or on related phenomena. In such a search we might find a variety of conditions to be extant. There might be very little theory, a great deal of theory, theory inadequately tested, theory poorly developed, a series of untested hypotheses, poorly developed concepts, limited empirical data, and

---

[4] Russell L. Ackoff, *The Design of Social Research*, The University of Chicago Press, Chicago, 1953, p. 14.

so on. On the basis of what we find, we can proceed to determine what is known about organizational behavior that would be pertinent to explaining the behavior of executives in medium-sized companies. At the extremes, we could find a very well-developed theory, dealing in detail with the behavior of executives in the medium-sized companies or, on the other hand, find virtually no theory at all dealing with organizational behavior.

Theoretical Framework. The researcher, drawing upon the review of the existing knowledge plus, of course, his own knowledge and experience, is ready to set forth what is known as the theoretical framework for the proposed study. In this theoretical framework he will indicate, for example, the basic conceptual scheme, theory or theories, hypotheses, models, and assumptions within which he plans to conduct the study.

As was stated previously, the same phenomena can usually be conceptualized in different ways, even within the same discipline. We can study the same phenomena from different theoretical viewpoints. The purpose of setting forth the theoretical framework is to indicate explicitly the particular viewpoint within which the study will be conducted. By preparing the framework as carefully as possible, the investigator will be able to effectively focus his study. He will have a valuable device to guide data collection and analysis as well as to communicate to others his orientation.

Where theory has been well developed and tested, the theoretical framework may simply summarize the theory and possibly give the hypotheses based on the theory which are to be tested by the study. At the other extreme, the investigator, in lieu of theory, may give a series of assumptions and conclusions drawn from these assumptions. He will, in effect, find himself cutting a new theory from whole cloth. Typically, the theoretical framework is based on something between these two extremes.

The particular approach to be used in setting forth the theoretical framework can vary considerably. In some cases it may be prepared as a section distinct from the review of existing knowledge, while in others it may be woven in with the review. However it is done, it is really quite critical that the investigator explicitly set forth the orientation of his study. By making it explicit he will be in a good position to deliberately and carefully examine its logic. If the orientation is implied rather than stated, he will not be as likely to rigorously review its logic nor be in as good a position to do so.

Problem Formulation. Following the review of existing knowledge and development of the theoretical framework, the researcher can then proceed to formulate the problem to be solved in accomplishing the purpose of the study and to argue for the particular formulation which he has evolved. The argument will be made in terms of—and rest on—the theory and assumptions. He may decide that the next logical task in the development of a theory should be to test hypotheses, and he will argue this logical step. On the other hand, he may decide the next step will be to re-evaluate the conceptual scheme of the theory, analyze the logic of existing theory, or reconsider inferences from empirical knowledge.

The formulation of a research problem is typically published with the results of the research. It probably differs from the original formulation in the research design, since it has the benefit of the completed research, but examples can illustrate the character of problem analysis.

J. Johnston in his book *Statistical Cost Analysis* [5] reports on some empirical work which he did to test hypotheses that are drawn from economic theory and deal with cost. In the first part of his book he summarizes a review of economic theory. He titles the chapter in which he does this "Theoretical Hypotheses about the Relationships between Costs and Output." He refers to a number of basic ideas and to the work of economists who have developed or done some work on ideas in this particular area of economic theory. He then formulates the problem to be solved by his research.

Another example to illustrate this idea of careful evaluation of existing theory to provide the basis for research is an article by Karl Brunner and Allan H. Meltzer, in the field of money and banking, "Predicting Velocity: Implications for Theory and

---

[5] J. Johnston, *Statistical Cost Analysis*, McGraw-Hill Book Co., 1960.

Policy." [6] The following sentences quoted from their review of current theory provide a good insight into this methodology.

It has become commonplace for economists to say, "The quantity theory of money, M equals kY, holds only, if at all, in the long run. The ratio of money per unit of income, or its reciprocal, income velocity, is subject to substantial short-run fluctuation. The model is at best a useful long-run approximation." As yet there is no accepted theoretical explanation of the short-run behavior of velocity, which is to say that there is no theory of the demand function for money that is sufficiently in accord with the observed short-run behavior of velocity to be useful for prediction and that explains relatively constant long-run velocity.

Recent theoretical work has suggested a promising reformulation of monetary and macroeconomic theory in terms of the demand and supply functions for assets.

Indeed, the general concept of a wealth-adjustment process has yielded two (approximative) macroeconomic theories.

These differences in approach challenge economists to provide evidence capable of distinguishing between alternative theories.

In recent papers, we have attempted to formulate and test demand and supply functions for money and to compare our results to existing alternative theories.

Of particular relevance for this paper is the work on the demand function for money or the velocity relation.

These results seem to support the view taken above that the formulation of macroeconomic theory which emphasizes the demand and supply functions for money provides more stable relations than alternative approaches that stress the demand and supply for real capital or are based on flows.[7]

After the authors have completed their review of theory, they then proceed to set forth their formulation of the problem which they sought to study in the project. They say in part:

---

[6] Karl Brunner and Allan H. Meltzer, "Predicting Velocity: Implications for Theory and Policy," *The Journal of Finance*, Vol. XVIII, No. 2, May, 1963, p. 319.

[7] *Ibid.*, pp. 319–321.

In this paper the problem of predicting velocity in the short run is reopened. The predictive performance of the wealth model is compared with the performance of a number of alternative theories of the demand for money to obtain both relative and absolute measures of the power of the various demand-for-money or velocity relations *in the short run*.[8]

A study which reports on work which sought not so much to test ideas drawn from existing theory but rather to develop new concepts and new theory is *Organizations* [9] by James G. March and Herbert A. Simon. The book begins with a review of existing theoretical developments and indicates their weaknesses. Then it proceeds to set forth a new approach and argue for its value over traditional theory. The following list of topics appears in the first two chapters of the book and indicates the author's approach:

Chapter 1 Organizational Behavior
  1.1 The Significance of Organizations as Social Institutions
  1.2 The Literature of Organization Theory
  1.3 Organization of this Book
  1.4 Some Types of Propositions
  1.5 Some Psychological Postulates

Chapter 2 "Classical" Organization Theory
  2.1 Taylor's Scientific Management
  2.2 Theories of Departmentalization
  2.3 Operational and Empirical Problems of Classical Administrative Science
  2.4 Conclusion

PROBLEM ANALYSIS—APPLIED RESEARCH

The process of problem analysis varies somewhat between problem-solving research and basic research. Since applied research focuses on the development of knowledge to manipulate some aspects of the environment, problem analysis is conducted within the framework of operational tasks and objectives. Problem analysis in an inventory system study will very likely be concerned

---

[8] *Ibid.*, p. 322.
[9] James G. March and Herbert A. Simon, *Organizations,* John Wiley and Sons, New York, 1958, p. ix.

with increasing inventory control rather than the theoretical understanding of inventories (although this could be a by-product). In basic research, problem analysis revolves around finding and properly stating significant questions to be answered to increase understanding of phenomena.

Review of Existing Knowledge. As in basic research, problem analysis involves a review of existing knowledge. This includes theoretical knowledge pertinent to the phenomena involved. It can include theory from more than one discipline if the theory provides needed understanding. This is one rather significant difference from basic research which will typically be concerned with the development of theory from the point of view of a single discipline or field. Review of existing knowledge in basic economic research will tend to emphasize the theoretical work in economics, although this approach is often too narrow even in basic research of a science. Applied research to improve the administration of production could draw on theory from sociology, cultural anthropology, psychology, and political science. Since the purpose is to review any theory which might increase understanding of the behavior of people as individuals and in groups, theory from any discipline studying human behavior might be pertinent.

In addition to a review of theory, problem analysis in applied research also includes a review of proposed and successful solutions for the same or similar problems. If the study concerns itself with optimizing inventory ordering, the review would include a consideration of solutions that others have developed for this problem. The review would also consider other techniques that have been developed and are pertinent to the problem. Techniques for economic forecasting, for example, might prove pertinent as well as methods for evaluating investments.

Theoretical Framework. In setting forth the theoretical framework, the investigator will (as in basic research) indicate the basic conceptual scheme and the theory that will guide the research plus assumptions to supplement theory or in lieu of theory. Assumptions may also be included about the state of phenomena as well as the nature of phenomena. The theoretical framework will provide the understanding and/or assumption about phenomena that will guide the researcher in his efforts to develop methods and techniques to aid in the manipulation of phenomena and thus lead to problem solving.

If the study seeks to evaluate the feasibility of a proposed salt-water aquarium site, the theoretical framework might consist of a series of statements about the nature of the economy of salt-water aquariums, about customers who attend salt-water aquariums, and possibly a series of assumptions about the specific site and environment proposed for the aquarium. These could be assumptions about the local tourist trade and the recreation habits of local citizens, for example.

The theoretical framework will, to use again Toulmin's analogy, set forth a map which indicates the nature of the landscape plus some assumptions about the state of the landscape. The researcher's problem will then be to decide what needs to be done to devise an itinerary for the proposed trip, using the map and his additional assumptions.

By explicitly setting forth his theoretical framework, the investigator will be in a better position to determine the approach to solving operational problems than if the theory and assumptions of his research are left implicit. As in basic research, he will also be in a better position to examine his logic and communicate his orientation to others.

Problem Formulation. By relying on all information which has been collected, the researcher may then formulate the problem or problems to be solved in accomplishing the purpose of the study. If theory indicates that the best approach to analyzing the economics of production is in terms of incremental costs, the problem could be to devise a technique to measure or estimate incremental costs at various levels of production. If theory and/or assumptions indicate that a neighborhood bank's demand deposits are dependent on the physical appearance of the bank and its proximity to general shopping and parking convenience, the problem would center on measuring these concepts and their relationships.

A very interesting turn of events can take place when the researcher decides that, before the operational problem can be solved, additional work must be done in the area of theory. Existing theory and concepts may not be appropriate for his problem. If this possibility occurs, the researcher could make the decision to do additional work in the area of theory. Conceivably, therefore, what set out to be an applied research design could develop a problem formulation very similar to what a basic researcher might have done.

Finding examples illustrating problem analysis in applied research is somewhat more difficult than basic research. The practice in reporting basic research requires that the author indicate the theory and analysis underlying his research. Since applied research places emphasis on the problem to be solved, reports emphasize the problem and the solution and minimize attention to a review of existing knowledge, theoretical and operational.

Books on managerial economics offer illustrations of efforts to offer solutions to operational problems based on theory. For example, they typically analyze the problem to be solved in estimating demand in terms of demand theory and techniques for measuring the concepts set forth in demand theory. Spencer and Siegelman say, "For the most part the problem consists of bridging the gap between the concept of demand as it exists in economic theory and the measurement of demand by statistical methods." [10] Joel Dean and William W. Haynes, in their respective books on managerial economics,[11] discuss demand theory at some length and then review techniques for identifying concepts drawn from theory.

Bierman, Fouraker, and Jaedicke, in *Quantitative Analysis for Business Decisions,* discuss at some length probability theory, then use it in the development of a variety of techniques for problem solving. Earlier in this book a reference was made to a technique which they developed based on probability theory and economic theory. Another illustration relating theory to problem solving was their analysis of costs. They suggest the use of probability analysis for cost control.

[10] Milton H. Spencer and Louis Siegelman, *Managerial Economics,* Richard D. Irwin, Homewood, Illinois, 1959, p. 135.

[11] Joel Dean, *Managerial Economics,* Prentice-Hall, Inc., Englewood Cliffs, New Jersey, 1951, and William Warren Haynes, *Managerial Economics, Analysis and Cases,* The Dorsey Press, Homewood, Illinois, 1963.

The procedure to be suggested here will use some concepts from probability theory and statistics. Basically, the procedure will be to determine the *probability distribution* of each cost for different levels of activity. Based on this distribution, acceptable ranges for cost deviations can then be established.[12]

RESEARCH STRATEGY

Once the investigator has formulated his problem, he is then ready to consider the general approach which he is going to take to solve the problem and, following this decision, select the specific techniques and tools which will be appropriate. Since the same techniques can be used or deployed in different ways, it is of considerable help to the investigator to consider carefully his general approach to a research project before he considers the tools and techniques.

Once an architect has decided on the problems to be solved in the construction of a house, he can then consider the type of house that will be most appropriate in meeting these needs and, second, the particular techniques to be used in construction. Many of the same methods, materials, techniques, and tools can be used in the construction of houses of different architectural style. Logically, the architect will first decide on the type of house to be built—colonial, early American, contemporary, modern. After his decision on the style, he can then proceed with the details of the house and the techniques for its construction.

There are a variety of classifications that could be suggested to illustrate research strategies which could be used. One possibility would be to consider an empirical approach versus a nonempirical approach. If the researcher were evaluating the logic of a theory or comparing the conclusions of two theories, a nonempirical approach might be useful. Attempting to analyze theory to develop new hypotheses would also suggest a non-empirical strategy. Testing hypotheses or evaluating a method to predict events would both require empirical analysis.

Books on research methods and techniques frequently suggest

---

[12] Bierman, Fouraker, and Jaedicke, *op. cit.*, p. 111.

categories for considering research strategies. Festinger and Katz, in *Research Methods in the Behavioral Sciences*,[13] discuss the problem in four chapters under the heading "Research Settings." The chapter titles are:

The Sample Survey: A Technique for Social Science Research
Field Studies
Experiments in Field Settings
Laboratory Experiments

They follow these four chapters with a discussion of various techniques which can be used in social science research.

Selltiz, Jahoda, Deutsch, and Cook, in *Research Methods in Social Relations*,[14] discuss two research strategies before they undertake a review of various research techniques: "Research Design: I Exploratory and Descriptive Studies" and "Research Design: II Studies Testing Causal Hypotheses."

Other possible examples would include: construction of a computer simulation, analysis of records and documents, introspective exploration to develop new concepts, preparation of a report or a description, and analysis of the internal logic of a theory or problem-solving technique.

There is no all-purpose classification of research strategies. The appropriateness of various strategies will vary from field to field and from problem to problem. The researcher in his plan must, however, carefully consider what general approach will be most appropriate for his particular investigation, given: the nature of the problem, the limits of time and money, the general level of knowledge, plus many other restrictions. This aspect of research planning needs to be carefully considered to insure a sound basis for the selection of the specific techniques and tools that will be used.

Ackoff's book, *Scientific Method: Optimizing Applied Research Decisions,* is essentially devoted to dealing with this prob-

---

[13] Leon Festinger and Daniel Katz, editors, *Research Methods in the Behavioral Sciences*, The Dryden Press, New York, 1953.

[14] Claire Selltiz, Marie Jahoda, Morton Deutsch, and Stuart W. Cook, *Research Methods in Social Relations*, Holt, Rinehart, and Winston, Inc., New York, 1959.

lem of deciding on the best method to tackle a problem and on the approach for selecting techniques and tools.

By a scientific *method* we refer to the way techniques are selected in science; that is, to the evaluation of alternative courses of scientific action. Thus, whereas the techniques used by a scientist are results of his *decisions,* the way these decisions are made is the result of his *decision rules.* Methods are rules of choice; techniques are the choices themselves. For example, a procedure for selecting the best of a set of possible sampling designs is a scientific method; and the selection of the most suitable of a set of alternative ways of measuring a property, such as length, hardness, intelligence, or cooperation, involves the use of a method.

The study of scientific methods is frequently referred to as *methodology.* The objective of methodology is the improvement of the procedures and criteria employed in the conduct of scientific research. For this reason, methodology is often referred to as the logic of *science.*

In this book our concern will be primarily with the methods of science rather than with its techniques and tools. First, the various phases of research activity will be identified, phases which are involved either implicitly or explicitly in every research project. Then the methodology of each phase will be considered.[15]

RESEARCH TECHNIQUES

The research design begins to take on detailed focus as the researcher selects the particular techniques which he will use in solving the problem he has formulated and in carrying out the strategy which he has selected. If he has decided to use a survey, he then needs to select the devices to be used in conducting the survey. Included will be the techniques to be used in collecting the data and in its analysis. He could, for example, use an open-ended questionnaire, a quota sample, and correlation analysis.

If someone were interested in using the experimental approach to studying organizational behavior, he might devise a business game as a device to collect information. He could then have a sample of people play the game. Several statistical techniques could be used to analyze his results.

---

[15] Ackoff, *op. cit.,* p. 6.

Some of the research techniques most familiar to business researchers for collecting information include the open- and closed-end questionnaires, tests and examinations, sampling, observation, and collecting information from records. Examples of analytical techniques would include correlation, analysis of variance, content analysis, and linear programming.

There are a number of books available on techniques for collecting and analyzing data, and there is some specialization between the various fields in business. Marketing research tends to have more interest in tools to study human behavior than accounting. If one seeks to become a proficient researcher, he needs to become well acquainted with research techniques in his field plus those techniques developed in other fields that could be transferred to his. Psychology, sociology, and anthropology have developed a number of techniques which can prove quite useful in several fields of business administration.

The experienced researcher also needs to appreciate the theory which underlies research techniques. Statistics offers a very good illustration. The discipline of statistics has developed an extensive body of theory which underlies its work. Some of this has been drawn from mathematics. To become efficient in the use of statistics, the researcher needs to become well acquainted not only with the use of statistics in the analyses of data but also with the underlying theory of the various analytical devices. The effective use of sampling, widely applied in the collection of data, depends on a sound understanding of probability. The proper use of questionnaires depends on an understanding of the problem of human communication and human behavior. To become efficient in business research, therefore, he needs not only to know theory concerning the phenomena which he is studying but also the theory underlying the various techniques which he may use in conducting his research.

FORMAT OF FINDINGS

Although the format in which the results will be presented may often be obvious, it is well for the researcher in preparing his research design to consider the specific method he will use to present his findings. If the research is applied, he may want to consider the preparation of a manual—rather than just a report —which can be used as a guide by those who will be applying the findings of the study. Another possibility would be the preparation of more than one version of the report for different audiences or different purposes—a prose report and algorithm programmed for a computer.

A statement of the proposed format of the research will make it clear to others what can be expected from the study. This can be especially important if the research is applied and is being done for a client or supervisor who has more interest in the output of the research than in how the results are secured.

TIME SCHEDULE AND BUDGET

A final step often included in a research design, particularly one which is being used to support a request for a grant or an appropriation, is a proposed budget and time schedule. The usefulness of this step can serve both as a guide in the allocation of limited funds and time and as an argument to support the need for both, particularly funds. Schedules and budgets are both standard planning devices and their use in preparing a research design is really quite similar to their use in any other type of planning. Their extensiveness will tend to be related to the size of the resources to be used or needed. It is not very likely that a graduate student would prepare a detailed time table for his work in developing a term paper—or would his research design be detailed. An extensive project involving large sums of money, however, would require detailed planning and a correspondingly detailed budget.

CONCLUSION

This discussion has reviewed the basic aspects of planning a research project using a specific sequence, but this does not necessarily mean that a research project is always planned in such a sequence. It is difficult in planning a project not to consider, as we attempt to evaluate the problem to be solved, the techniques available to the researcher. If a computer is available, he may decide to formulate a problem in a somewhat different way than if he had to proceed without it. The investigator may prefer one theoretical framework for the study over another, but he may not be able to use it because the concepts involved simply cannot be measured satisfactorily. Time and funds may also place severe limits on how the problem is formulated. In the development of a research design, therefore, there is an interplay involved between the various aspects of the design. Although the researcher may begin with a specific theory and a set of concepts, his thinking will be modified as he considers other aspects of the project.

Another fact which needs to be emphasized is that the reseach design is a first approximation. It is an attempt to begin the research project drawing upon existing knowledge and the best thinking available. Once the project is underway, the reseacher may very well wish to reconsider his assumptions. He may want to reformulate his problem. He may find that his basic strategy or some of the techniques which he at first thought would be appropriate are, for some reason or other, inadequate. But this can be said of any plan. A plan to construct a bridge may have to be altered when work has begun on the pilings. It may be discovered that certain vital information was not available when the plan was prepared, and thus a change must be made.

TABLE 4   Research Design Outline

   I. Topic
  II. Purpose of study
 III. Problem analysis
     A. Summary of current knowledge pertinent to topic
        1. Concepts, theories, principles, etc.
        2. Empirical findings
        3. Reports and descriptions
        4. Suggested hypotheses
        5. Evaluation of current knowledge
        6. Existing and proposed solutions to operational problems
     B. Theoretical framework of study
        1. Concepts and theory to be used in study
        2. Assumptions of study—theoretical and empirical
     C. Detailed statement of the problem to be solved to achieve objectives of study

IV. Research strategy to be used
V. Research techniques to be used
VI. Format for reporting results of study
VII. Time schedule and budget
VIII. Bibliography of materials used in preparing research design

6

Models

One of the most effective methods that has ·been developed for studying relationships within a conceptual scheme is the use of a technique that will in some way represent or depict the relationships and, specifically, the form which they take. Such a technique is the model, a familiar and well-known tool of science. It has proven extremely helpful in studying and analyzing both ideas and empirical observations.

TYPES OF MODELS

Probably the most familiar model is the "iconic model" which looks like what it seeks to represent. An example would be a scale model of an airplane built to study a new concept in designing airplanes. Such a scale model will give some indication of the relationship between various parts of the aircraft's body—fuselage, wings, or stabilizer, for instance. If the model is properly built, it can be placed in a wind tunnel to simulate the flight of the proposed aircraft. A concept for building locks to raise and lower ships in a canal can be studied by building a scale model of the locks, the canal, and the ships which will ply the canal. If the model is built with moving parts, not only will it look like what it seeks to represent, but it can also simulate to some extent the operation of the proposed system. Iconic models would also include statues, photographs, and other facsimiles. The only requirement of an iconic model is that it should look like what it represents.

Another type of model is the "analog" which, although it does not look like what it represents, behaves in a similar manner. An analog model of an eclipse of the moon could be made by focusing a flashlight on a ball and casting a shadow on this ball by passing a second ball between it and the light. The balls do not look like either the earth or the moon and the flashlight does not look like the sun, but the three have certain characteristics in common with the three bodies to allow their use to simulate an eclipse. An analog model of a rectangular parking lot could be made by a scale drawing of a rectangle. The length and width of individual cars could be represented by sections of cardboard cut to scale. These pieces of cardboard, templates, could then be placed on the drawing to simulate cars parked on the lot. Neither the drawing nor the cardboard templates look like the parking lot or the cars but they do simulate certain aspects of both. This analog model will allow one to study the relationships between the width and length of the cars and the space provided by the parking lot. A similar type of analog model to study factory layouts would be templates representing equipment arranged on a scale drawing of the available floor space. Another example of an analog model is the familiar blueprint. A well-known one in economics is the chart and the use of lines to represent relationships between or among concepts.

Yet another type of model is the "symbolic model" which uses symbols to represent the phenomena being studied. In studying production costs, T might represent total costs, U the number of units produced, and UC the cost per unit. The symbolic model to represent the relationships would be $T/U = UC$. In a situation where variable costs increase by \$20 with each increase of 100 units in production, a symbolic model representing the relationship and indicating total cost could be written as follows: $TC = FC + 20x$. FC would be fixed cost and x the number of groups of 100 units which are produced. Typically, symbolic models take on the form of mathematical equations.

Possibly another type of model might be suggested and could be referred to as the "verbal model." A verbal model might be defined as one that relies on verbal expressions to represent the concepts involved and to indicate the form of the regularity. For example, the variations from standard cost over the twelve-month period are normally distributed. If we cannot use any other approach to building a model, we can attempt to indicate the form of the regularity verbally. In fact, it may be that in many cases before we can build an iconic, symbolic, or analog model, it may first be necessary to develop a verbal model. An analytical report written in prose which discusses concepts and indicates the form of the regularity involved would constitute a verbal model. The criteria of whether or not a prose report can be considered to be a model would be whether or not it deals with the patterns and regularities and their form. In the social sciences, where it is frequently difficult to find techniques to build an analog or symbolic model, there is often no alternative but to report research in prose. If the report indicates the form of relationships prevailing, it can be considered a model, a verbal model. This type of a report would be distinguished from one that simply classifies and reports facts, but does not seek to single out regularities and indicate their form.

These various models, though quite different, all illustrate the basic purpose and function of models. They abstract specific concepts from the environment, which are sometimes referred to as the components or the variables of the model, and depict the way in which these concepts are related. A photograph of a person's face is an abstraction from the totality of the person. A great deal is excluded. The only aspects of the person included are the face, and the components of the model are the various features of the face. The photograph, as a model, indicates something of the relationship between the various components of the face. Templates for cars and a scale drawing of a parking lot area give models which abstract from the parking lot the concepts of length and width, excluding all other aspects. These concepts of length and width depicted by the templates and the parking lot drawing are the components of the model, and the relationships are implied in moving the templates about the drawing. The symbols of the symbolic model represent the components of the model which have been extracted from the total phenomena and the functions of the symbolic model will indicate the form of the relationship. In the symbolic model $TC = FC + 20x$, TC, FC, and x are the components of the model, and the indicated operations of addition and multiplication show the form of the relationship as well as the constant, 20.

MODELS, CONCEPTS AND RELATIONSHIPS

Since the purpose of the model is the representation of relationships between or among concepts, the prerequisite for any model building is a conceptual scheme and either information or assumptions about patterns and relationships. The value of the model will depend upon the appropriateness of the conceptual scheme for regarding the phenomena of interest. If we were interested in building a model of the business firm or some aspects of the firm, we need to begin with a conceptual scheme and one which is appropriate. This is an important question that is easily overlooked. The temptation is simply to select a conceptual scheme which is reasonably well known and proceed from that point. If we were interested in building a model to depict the relationships in the area of cost, we could use traditional conceptual frameworks in accounting or economics. The problem will be to select the appropriate one, and it may well develop that neither the accounting nor economic framework is appropriate. It may be more satisfactory to use a framework from sociology or at least to introduce some concepts from sociology. This could be the case if we were studying cost and the behavior of people under different cost conditions.

Principle sources of conceptual schemes for model building will be theories, laws, hypotheses, and principles, and the appropriateness of the model will depend upon the appropriateness of the theory, for example, from which the conceptual schemes were drawn. Models are not substitutes for conceptual schemes, principles, hypotheses, or theories but rather are devices to depict their concepts and the relationships which are involved; they are particularly concerned with the form of the relationships. If the concepts of a theory are poorly defined or are difficult to measure, a model drawn from the theory will suffer from this weakness. If a theory offers an explanation for a very limited aspect of phenomena, the model will be limited by this characteristic. If we think of theory as a group of verbal models (axioms and theorems), simply translating them into symbolic or mathematical models does not necessarily overcome weaknesses such as poorly defined concepts. It does, however, more clearly state the relationship and makes the statements of theory more susceptible to analysis.

Since a model is designed to depict relationships, it follows that if a conceptual scheme is designed only to classify observations, there is no need for a model; and in fact, a model cannot be built because there is no information on the relationships existing between or among the concepts being used to classify phenomena. A model cannot be built within a scheme used just to classify firms. If the concepts are the total sales, number of employees, and geographic location, and the scheme is used only to classify, it will not provide information on relationships; and hence a model could not be built. On the other hand, if a relationship were to be discovered between or among the concepts, it would then become feasible to build a model. If it were discovered that there were a relationship between the total sales and geographic location, a model could then be built if it were also possible to determine the form of the relationship.

If we were going to use a model to study advertising, we could begin with the hypothesis: as advertising expenditures are increased, sales will increase. Our concepts might be defined as follows: advertising, expenditures per month and sales, total sales per month. If we wish to build a symbolic model, we could select symbols to represent each of these concepts:

$$X = \text{advertising expenditures per month}$$
$$Y = \text{total sales per month}$$

The next step would seek to incorporate patterns. The model builder would need to determine the form of the relationship and see if there is a technique available to depict it. If the relationship turns out to be a linear one, he might find that the relationship between Y and X could be depicted by the form $Y = a + bX$ and the final model might be $Y = \$10,000 + 50X$. Every dollar spent on advertising returns $50 in sales.

It may develop, however, that the hypotheses and hence the conceptual scheme with which the model builder started was not very satisfactory. It may not have been satisfactory because he

THE HUNT LIBRARY
CARNEGIE INSTITUTE OF TECHNOLOGY

could not develop definitions and measures for sales and advertising that would lead to satisfactory data collection. If, however, he were able to develop these measures, he might find that no stable patterns existed; and hence he could not build a stable model. Both of these problems could mean that the conceptual scheme was not complete or that an entirely different framework was needed for building a model to study advertising. Possibly a second hypothesis could be added incorporating types of advertising and customer attitudes.

MODEL BUILDING

Based on a conceptual scheme and on information or assumptions about relationships, the task in building a model is to select or develop a technique to represent the concepts and to depict the form of the relationship prevailing between or among the components.

In building an iconic model of an automobile body, the components would be such items as the hood and fenders, and these could be represented with clay, wood, plastic, or even metal. The form of the relationship between the components could be assumed by visual inspection or determined through careful measurement. The model would abstract from the total car only those concepts dealing with the body excluding, for example, the motor, interior trim, and transmission. A very simple device for depicting the concepts and the form of relationship in developing an iconic model of a car body would be a photograph. This approach, of course, could not be used in attempting to build an iconic model to depict some ideas which one might be proposing for the construction of automobile bodies.

One of the principal purposes in building a model is the development of a device to analyze the relationships. On this basic point iconic models have serious limitations. Typically, it is not possible to manipulate the concepts to study the effect that a change in one will have on the others. We might be interested in the effect of increasing the size of the fender or flattening the hood. In an iconic model this cannot be done unless it is made in a manner that will allow this. If the model were made of soft clay, this would be possible; or if it were made of metal with removable parts so that different fender concepts could be inserted into the model. The iconic model is also weak, in that it does not depict explicitly the form of the relationship, but rather it depicts it implicitly. The width of the fender compared to the hood is implied but not specifically set forth.

If we are not primarily interested in using a model to study the form of the relationships prevailing between or among the concepts, but rather in some overall use of a model which is based on an accurate depiction of the relationship, the iconic model can be very satisfactory. An iconic model of an airplane can be used very effectively in a wind tunnel to simulate the flight of the proposed aircraft. The iconic model of an automobile body could be helpful in evaluating the aesthetic effects. Usually, however, a model is needed which allows us to manipulate the components and that indicates the form of the relationship explicitly.

The analog model offers a more satisfactory technique for analysis than does the iconic model. In building an analog model the investigator is free to use methods which will provide a device that behaves in some respects similar to the phenomena being studied even though they do not look like it. This introduces considerable flexibility and opportunity to the model builder. He can use devices that will allow him to manipulate the components of the model. Like the iconic model, however, the analog model indicates the form of the relationship implicitly rather than explicitly.

A template being used to represent a piece of machinery will have dimensions, length and width such as the machinery, but it will not in any way look like the equipment. It will have two characteristics of the equipment which are the only aspects of interest in the analysis. By using a template and a floor design, we can simulate the effect on floor space of placing the machinery in various locations. With a graph or chart, we can depict the relationship between cost and production by a line. By projecting the trend of the line, we are actually studying the effect on one variable when another is changed.

The symbolic model is at a higher level of abstraction than either the iconic or analog model and is more explicit in dealing with the form of the relationships. The symbolic model typically uses letters, numerals, and mathematical functions to depict concepts and relationships. If we are dealing with width and length, the letters W and L could be used to represent the two concepts. If it is discovered that in some particular situations length tends to be ten times greater than width, we could set up the following model: $L = 10W$. This model depicts a very limited aspect of a phenomena but indicates very explicitly the form of the relationship. An iconic model has the advantage of being able to depict many aspects of a phenomenon; but it is not explicit about the relationship, while the symbolic model usually deals with more limited aspects of the environment but is explicit about the form of the relationships. The symbolic model is the most satisfactory of the various types of models, if we seek an analytic model. Since it is usually stated in a mathematical form, the symbolic model can be more effectively manipulated than the other types of models. A problem in using the symbolic model in the social sciences is the difficulty of determining the form of a regularity observed with adequate precision and finding an appropriate technique to depict the regularity.

MATHEMATICS AND MODEL BUILDING

Without any doubt, model building, any kind of model, is an art and depends upon the ingenuity, skill, and training of the model builder. If we wish to use models as techniques of analysis, a prerequisite is to acquaint ourselves with methods that have been used in their construction. If we are interested in building models to represent ideas from an aesthetic standpoint—new concepts in automobile bodies or commercial buildings—we would want to study those methods which will most effectively accomplish this goal.

In a great deal of scientific research, the goal has been to build models that can be used to analyze the relationship between and among concepts rather than to build models to consider aesthetic effects. As a result, the most satisfactory models tend to be analog or symbolic models. The typical introductory textbook in economics, for example, is full of charts (analog models) representing various economic relationships. In recent years economics has been increasing the emphasis on the use of symbolic models.

Because of their value as analytic devices of considerable power, both analog and symbolic models, especially symbolic models, have proven most helpful. The physicists have been so successful in using symbolic models that a physicist is often as good a mathematician as he is a physicist. In business administration, operations research and management science have increased the emphasis on the use of symbolic models and have built some very effective ones. The emphasis on the use of symbolic models has also been increasing throughout the social sciences.

One of the most useful sources of model-building techniques discovered in scientific research is mathematics both for building analog and symbolic models but principally symbolic. Mathematics is concerned with the study of relationships between or among abstract concepts which are not empirically oriented. Plane geometry offers a good example of the nature of mathematics as a tool for building both analog and symbolic models. Some of its basic concepts or basic elements of its conceptual scheme would include lines, points, angles, and various geometric designs such as triangles, circles, and quadrangles. Working with these basic structures or concepts, students of plane geometry seek to determine relationships and the form of the relationships prevailing. They do not, however, concern themselves with empirical definitions for its basic concepts. A point and line have no empirical definition. Within the framework they have studied, for example, the relationship among triangles, angles, and lines. One result of their efforts is the familiar Pythagorean theorem: the square of the hypotenuse of a right triangle is equal to the sum of the squares of the other two sides.

Algebra offers an example of a somewhat more abstract structure than geometry. It deals with the equations, symbols, and operations of adding, subtracting, dividing, and multiplying. Algebra, which involves work with the equation and nonnumerical symbols as well as with numerals, offers a very sophisticated study of relationships and a complex set of theorems concerning relationships. The abstractness and the empirical irrelevance of algebra is suggested by the fact that it is possible to engage in algebraic study without any reference to the empirical world.

We can get an insight into the nature of mathematics possibly through comparing it with the game of checkers. The game of checkers is a structure within an arbitrary framework consisting of the checkerboard, checkers, and rules for moving the checkers. Within this framework, we can study relationships and regularities and develop a rather sophisticated knowledge of relationships. The structure of checkers, however, is not related to the empirical world but is quite arbitrary. Although physical objects such as the checkerboard and the checkers are involved, their individual nature is not important. Their physical dimensions, for example, are not pertinent to the play of the game. Chess offers another example. In this case the concepts and rules are more complicated, and hence the study of chess can be more sophisticated because of the possibility of greater variation in patterns and relationships. In both games the player can, if he wishes, alter the game and turn it into another game without regard to the empirical world. Plane geometry similarly can change its structure and add a third dimension, creating solid geometry. With the new concept, we have a new set of mathematical concepts and rules and a new branch of mathematics. By adding several operations to algebra, we can convert it into calculus.

A pure mathematician is not concerned in his work with empirical observations but rather with creating abstract structures and working within these structures. He does not study natural phenomena. His testing of hypotheses and his establishment of theory is not the same type of activity as that of the empirical scientist. He establishes his knowledge through deductive analysis.

It can, of course, be argued that the environment of a mathematician may contribute to his work through suggesting structure. Lines and angles in the environment of man may have suggested some of the basic concepts of plane geometry. This does not mean, however, that plane geometry is an empirical study. The inventions of concepts in mathematics is a process of innovation and creation and like any creative work can be stimulated by experiences of the senses. The creations of art and music can also be stimulated by physical observations and experiences.

Although mathematics is not an empirical science and deals

with abstract relationships between nonempirical concepts, it has, however, proven quite useful to empirical science and for a most interesting reason. It has been discovered that the patterns and relationships found in mathematics often simulate quite closely those which have been found in the empirical world. The simulation is so close that people have sometimes concluded that the basic nature of the universe is mathematical in structure. Part of the explanation for the fact that mathematics tends to simulate patterns in the environment is the fact that the phenomenon itself has often been the basis for suggesting structures which have been built in mathematics. It is important, however, to distinguish between mathematical structures and patterns found in the phenomena, because we can be misled by the similarities discovered. Unwarranted conclusions can be drawn.

To illustrate the role that mathematics can play in simulating relationships, we might consider a situation where it has been found that with each additonal unit produced by a firm the cost goes up by a specified amount. Such a pattern can be simulated by a linear equation of the form $Y = a + bX$. When plotted on an arithmetic chart, it will give a straight line. If the linear equation correctly simulates the pattern for all the data available, it in effect is a technique for building a model to depict the pattern. The unwarranted conclusion that could be drawn would be to assume that the linear relationship holds for all levels of production. If there is sufficient empirical evidence to warrant the conclusion that the pattern holds for most levels of production, the model based on the linear mathematical form will prove a powerful tool. On the other hand, if the conclusion is unwarranted, the model will be limited. As more information becomes available, it may become apparent that—at certain levels of production—with each increase in production of one unit there may not always be a constant increase in cost. Furthermore in some cases cost might decline rather than increase. Therefore, to rely on the linear mathematical form to simulate the relationship might lead us to make predictions that later on might prove incorrect.

Another example might be drawn from a model to depict population studies. It may have been found that a certain population has been growing at a constant rate which could be depicted by the mathematical form $Y = ab^x$. This form, when plotted on a semi-logarithmic chart, will give a straight line. The problem of prediction will be one of determining under what conditions this mathematical form correctly depicts the pattern of population growth. This is a theoretical and empirical question and not a mathematical question.

The point of the discussion, therefore, is to note that mathematics is a discipline which has focused on the study of relationships between concepts which are not necessarily empirically oriented. The structure is artificial, in that it does not necessarily depict the nature of natural phenomena; and it is, therefore, important to note that although mathematics can frequently provide a structure that simulates phenomena in the natural environment, it does not follow that mathematics itself is expressing the truth about the natural environment. It is simply providing a tool that can be helpful in studying the natural environment. The nature of the natural environment will be discovered only through empirical observations and the development of hypotheses, theories and laws which can be tested empirically. As empirical knowledge is increased, it will become apparent to what extent the mathematical tools being used to simulate the patterns of the natural phenomena will provide a valid simulation.

The process, then, in the use of mathematics in model building will be somewhat the same as the use of any technique to depict the form of the regularity. Once we have an insight into the pattern, the problem is to find a technique to depict it. One approach is to look in the area of mathematical patterns to see if any of the forms satisfactorily depict the regularity. This is the same approach as looking for something to depict a regularity through building an iconic model. Is there some form that can be found that will accurately depict the regularity? In depicting the form of an automobile body, one approach would be to use modeling clay, which can give some very satisfactory approaches to building a model. It would be a mistake, though, to assume that the clay or the clay model state truths about the automobile body. The truth, if any, will be in the knowledge and theory represented by the clay and the model. Similarly, a linear mathematical form can depict accurately some patterns found in the natural environment, but it will not be the same as the natural environment. It will only simulate this environment and only in limited fashion.

The advantage of using mathematics to build models is that a mathematical model can be so easily manipulated, and there are so many mathematical forms to draw on in model building. These characteristics of mathematics, however, while providing such great flexibility in model building, create at the same time great hazards for the model builder. The flexibility in manipulating a mathematical model makes it possible to manipulate a model beyond reality. This pitfall is not so great in working, let us say, with a clay model because the limitations on manipulation are more obvious. Clay has certain characteristics which are different from steel, and so this places limitations on clay models to depict something made of steel. Similarly, mathematics may have certain characteristics which are different from the phenomena being studied and hence places a limitation on the manipulation of mathematical models; but the limitations are not as obvious as in the clay and steel contrast. If the linear equation $Y = a + bX$ seems to describe population growth for the period 1900 through 1960, by simple manipulation, we can predict population for 1970; but there is the problem that this mathematical form may not describe the population growth that is taking place during the decade of the 1960's.

Our consideration of the role of mathematics in model building emphasizes the importance of theory and concepts. Mathematics, like any model building technique, neither replaces theory or concepts nor is it the same thing as theory or concepts. It is a technique which can be used to depict ideas but is not a substitute. The value of the technique, therefore, depends on how valuable are the ideas which it depicts. If on sound theoretical basis it can be established that populations grow in a pattern which can be depicted by a linear equation, then the equation can reliably be used to forecast. If the equation is just an empirical fit and is not supported theoretically, then there is doubt about its value for forecasting purposes.

COMPUTER MODELS

Special attention should be given by the prospective model builder in business research to the electric computer as an aid. The properties of the computer lend themselves to the construction of some very sophisticated and complex models in business administration and in the social sciences—which has resulted in widespread use of the computer in research in these areas.

One of the problems in model construction in business and in the social sciences is finding a technique to adequately handle a large number of variables and lend itself to analysis. It is difficult enough to find one that will handle a large number of variables; but when this is done, there may result a mathematical equation or series of equations which virtually defy analysis because of the extensive computations involved. The electronic computer has contributed to the solution of some of these problems because of its ability to handle large numbers of variables and because of its speed in manipulation.

The typical model so often used in business and economic analysis is the chart, which is an analog model. It has proven helpful because it has properties which allow the relationship to be depicted both geometrically and algebraically; but a serious weakness is the limited number of variables which can be handled. Some have attempted to include a three-dimensional representation, but the serious limitation remains. An alternative to the chart and the geometric representation has been the construction of symbolic models using several aspects of mathematics, algebra, calculus, probability, and difference equations. As these models become complex, analysis and manipulation becomes very cumbersome and time consuming. The computer has solved much of this aspect of the problem because of its speed and ability to handle a complex series of mathematical statements. The computer itself does not improve the mathematics or the theory underlying the models but serves as a very useful tool of analysis and in this fashion can contribute to both.

The computer has been valuable both in handling analog-type models as well as symbolic ones. As mentioned earlier, the symbolic model depicts explicitly the form of the relationship, while the analog implies the relationship. Often, the analog model is used in research simply because it is not possible to determine the relationship explicitly between variables and build a symbolic model. In this situation the computer is proving most useful.

The use of the computer in the two methods can be illustrated by efforts to determine the probability of drawing an ace in a hand of bridge. One approach would be to construct a symbolic model incorporating probability and the other to simply deal a large enough number of bridge hands and empirically compute the probability. The computer can be used to undertake both approaches. The latter approach, often called computer simulation, is useful when we cannot undertake the first approach (sometimes known as an analytical solution), because it is either too complex or knowledge is simply not available to determine explicitly the form of the relationships.

The use of the computer to simulate, which is to operate analog-type models, has become quite widespread throughout the social sciences. The difficulty of determining the form of the relationship is very characteristic of all the social sciences as well as of business administration, and the alternative of building an analog model on a computer has proven to be a significant breakthrough in research.

A typical example of the approach is illustrated with several examples in *A Behavioral Theory of the Firm* [1] by Cyert and March. They refer, for example, to a simulation which the authors develop of the operations of a department in a department store. They secured information on the standard operating rules and procedures of the department and wrote a computer program based on these rules. The computer was programmed to follow these rules as though it were the department. (An example would be the rule for pricing merchandise.) The model could then be used to study the behavior of the department under various conditions. This was achieved by feeding information dealing with various situations into the computer, and then the output would represent what the department would have done,

---

[1] Richard M. Cyert and James G. March, *A Behavioral Theory of the Firm*, Prentice-Hall, Englewood Cliffs, N.J., 1963, Ch. 7.

using its standard procedures. Hoggatt and Balderston in the *Simulation of Market Processes* [2] report on a computer simulation of the West Coast Lumber Industry's marketing practices. After they determined the practices of the industry and programmed the computer accordingly, they used their simulation to test a series of hypotheses.

The technique of computer simulation of complex processes probably represents one of the most significant developments in business and social science research. The potential is not yet fully explored and is a challenge to the imagination. A psychologist, for example, has sought to simulate the human personality and human fantasy.

MODELS AND RESEARCH

The use of models in research can vary considerably. In a study of some specifically observed phenomena, we could build empirical models based on our observations. In studying the relationship between rest periods and production, we could seek to build an empirical model based on the observations in a particular work situation. If we were interested in studying the relationship between customers and a particular store, we could build a model to depict this particular situation. Such empirical models are of value in both applied and basic research.

In applied research they will deal with the specific problem at hand and allow rather specific analysis and prediction. If we are interested in increasing sales, an empirical model indicating the relationship between sales and customer behavior would be of immense value. If we discover that there is a specific relationship between sales and customers' average income and distance from the store, we may readily determine that there is no power in our hands to increase sales, or that the only alternative to increasing sales will be to move closer to the customers.

In basic research the empirical model will be closely related to experimental work. The empirical model can provide the basis

---

[2] Frederick E. Balderston and Austin C. Hoggatt, *Simulation of Market Processes*, Institute of Business and Economic Research, University of California, Berkeley, Calif., 1962.

from which the scientist may later seek to generalize. If the scientist seeks to study the general problem of the relationship between customers and window displays, he may set up a number of experiments, build a series of empirical models, and then attempt a generalized model. An example could be drawn from the field of physics. Several experiments could be conducted to study the fall of objects to the earth. After a series of experiments the physicist could generalize and indicate something of the pattern: the distance an object falls equals the product of half the acceleration rate and the time squared. The model would be $s = 16t^2$ (s represents distance t, time.) Economics has generalized that, as price declines, demand will increase and has frequently depicted this through an analog model, a chart.

Models can be used at the various levels of generalization. In studying a particular firm, we might find that there is a specific pattern revealed by comparing units of production and average cost per unit. If we were successful in expressing this relationship in a model, it would be an empirical model. Such an empirical model would prove useful in predicting the average unit cost of production at different levels of production and for determining at what level of production we could find the lowest unit cost for that particular firm; but this would have limited theoretical implications. After this discovery a number of additional firms in the same industry might be studied to examine the pattern revealed by comparing production and average unit cost. Although there may be variations found between firms, it may become apparent that the basic pattern is the same. The individual variations may be due to different ages of the equipment being used, different methods of accounting, or different techniques for scheduling production. If it can be established that the variations are due to local conditions, it may be possible to conclude that there is a general pattern throughout the industry in the relationship between production and unit cost. A model to express this general pattern would be a generalized model developed from a series of empirical models.

The model in our illustration could be generalized further if, after study, it was found that the pattern of relationships between unit cost and production found between firms in the particular industry studied, was also true of firms in other industries. In time it may be concluded that a general model indicating the relationship might be applicable to all manufacturing industries. In this way a very general model could be developed and, if it received sufficient acceptance, might come close to what some refer to as a law.

Models can, therefore, be useful in expressing relationships that are thought of as law or are sufficiently general to be thought of as rather broad principles. In the typical economic textbook we find such generalized models used to depict relationships which prevail rather widely. In the textbooks of any fairly well-developed discipline we find statements which have general applicability. Such statements might be thought of as verbal models, and if they could be expressed in some other forms such as a mathematical model, they could be more effectively analyzed.

The process of developing a theory, it will be recalled, involves setting up axioms or postulates from which theorems are deducted. If we wish to take advantage of model-building techniques in forming a theory, we could state the axioms in the form of symbolic models, and the theorems deduced from the axioms can also be expressed as models.

Opportunities for the use of model-building techniques can be found throughout applied research and the problem-solving process. It is a technique of sufficiently general importance to be a standard requirement of anyone seriously interested in research to improve problem solving by management.

The well-known business games built with the use of computers are an illustration of computer simulations of the environment within which the businessman finds himself operating. These models attempt to incorporate patterns and relationships drawn from the environment of business systems and of the systems themselves.

Illustrative of the possibilities of model building in applied research is the book *Mathematical Models and Methods in Marketing*[3] in which a number of models are discussed. There are

---

[3] Edited by Frank Bass and others, *Mathematical Models and Methods in Marketing*, Richard D. Irwin, Homewood, Ill., 1961.

models dealing with customer behavior, promotional efforts, sales forecasting, and inventory management.

Models can be used not only in research but also in developing research designs. The review of the literature, for example, constitutes a review of models that have been developed to explain some phenomena or to help solve an operational problem. The theoretical framework could be built around a single model treated as an hypothesis or treated as a formula to provide a solution; the problem of the study could be to identify the concepts of the model and determine the form of the relationship. If the model is accepted as a correct representation of phenomena, the study may simply be concerned with securing empirical data on the concepts: a model for estimating the size of inventory orders could fall into this category.

7

Words, Meaning, and Research

Critical to scientific research, applied or basic, is the satisfactory definition of concepts. Whether concepts are used to classify or to study patterns, regularities, and relationships, their meanings need to be made as clear as possible. Data collected through interviews asking people where they usually shop may yield somewhat useless results, because the word "usually" is not very precise. If the meaning of words used in a theory or hypothesis is vague and ambiguous, the meaning of the theory or hypothesis will be also. An hypothesis dealing with customer behavior is not testable unless the meaning of "customer behavior" and other basic words involved are carefully defined.

The word "capital" is an excellent example of a term with which we have to be very careful when conducting research. It means different things to different people. For many people the word refers to a sum of money available for investment. Accountants frequently define the word in terms of net investment in an enterprise. On the other hand, economists use the word when speaking of equipment used in production. Because of the variety of meanings associated with this word, it loses much of its usefulness for research purposes. Other words, such as "net assets," "producer's durable equipment," and "equity capital," are frequently substituted in order to achieve more precision.

It is fairly obvious that in preparing a research report, the meaning of basic terms should be clear so as to insure that the report will be properly understood. It is more important, however, that the meaning of basic terms be clear when the research itself is being conducted. If the meaning of terms is not clear to the reseacher, neither will the results of the research be clear.

DEFINITION AND SCIENTIFIC RESEARCH

Scientific research, therefore, to achieve precision in its work, seeks to define in a very careful and deliberate manner the exact meaning of key terms. This means much more than developing a dictionary definition. In fact, definitions found in dictionaries are as a rule too incomplete and imprecise to be of value for research purposes. The following dictionary definition of overhead would be inadequate for someone interested in doing research on overhead:

Those general charges or expenses, collectively, in any business which cannot be charged up as belonging exclusively to any particular part of the work or product, as rent, taxes, insurance, lighting, heating, accounting and other office expenses, and depreciation.[1]

There is no assurance that two people studying the expenses of a firm will, by using this definition, come up with the same figure for overhead expenses. Accountants are well experienced with this problem of securing a sufficiently complete definition of a term so that two people using the term will collect similar data. When comparing the overhead figures of several companies, the accountant must usually check carefully to determine whether or not the figures are comparable.

An illustration of an attempt to define a term carefully is the following statement by John Maynard Keynes in which he sought to indicate the precise meaning he associated with the term "involuntary unemployment."

Men are involuntarily unemployed if, in the event of a small rise in the price of wage-goods relatively to the money-wage, both the aggregate supply of labour willing to work for the current money-wage and the aggregate demand for it at that wage would be greater than the existing volume of employment.[2]

---

[1] Webster's *New International Dictionary of the English Language*, Second Edition, G. and C. Merriam Co., Springfield, Mass., 1956.
[2] John Maynard Keynes, *The General Theory of Employment Interest and Money*, Harcourt, Brace and World, Inc., New York, p. 15.

The Bureau of the Census in its report, 1958 *Census of Business,* defined the term "payroll, entire year" as follows:

Payroll includes salaries, wages, commissions, bonuses, vacation allowances, and the value of payments in kind (such as free meals, lodgings, etc.) paid during the year to all employees. Gratuities received by employees from patrons are not included. For corporations, it includes amounts paid to officers and executives; it does not include compensation of proprietors or of patrons of unincorporated businesses. Payroll is reported before deductions for Social Security, income tax, insurance dues, etc.[3]

The following is an attempt to indicate the meaning associated with the term standard costs, taken from a well-known accounting textbook:

Current standard costs are ideal cost of operations computed on the basis of standardized production procedures. They are computed (usually but not necessarily) before production through the analysis of the various elements that enter into the costs of operations.[4]

It is often not possible to indicate satisfactorily the meaning associated with a term in a sentence or two. None of the three examples of definitions just given would really be complete enough to guide research. If the meaning of a concept is rather complicated, it may be necessary to prepare a rather lengthy statement in order to set forth accurately the meaning involved. Such a statement not only may involve several paragraphs but several pages and possibly a book. A fairly long statement may be desirable because of the need to indicate not just the meaning of one term but of several related terms which together represent a fundamental idea. In his book, *World Resources and Industries,*[5] Eric W. Zimmermann—while indicating the meaning he associated with the term "resources"—in effect set forth a theory of resources, and in the process he discussed the meaning of several other terms such as nature, culture, resistances, technology, and

---

[3] Bureau of the Census, *1958 Census of Business,* Vol. 2, "Retail Trade-Area Statistics," U.S. Department of Commerce, Washington, D.C., p. 3.

[4] Charles F. Schlatter and William J. Schlatter, *Cost Accounting,* John Wiley and Sons, New York, 1957, pp. 513–514.

[5] Erich W. Zimmermann, *World Resources and Industries,* Harper and Brothers, New York, 1951.

their relationships with each other and with resources. Consequently, his statement on the meaning of resources involved several introductory chapters in the book. An example of an entire book devoted to analyzing the meaning of a term is the book, *Culture: A Critical Review of Concepts and Definitions*,[6] by A. L. Kroeber and Clyde Kluckhohn.

MEANING OF CONCEPT NOT IN ITS LABEL

The meaning of a concept is not to be found in the term which is its label, and this is a very important point. It is necessary in working with concepts to distinguish between words and the concepts for which the words are labels. Words and concepts are not the same thing. Meaning is not in words. Words are symbols which are attached to express concepts. They are not, however, the only type of label which can be given to concepts. We can use letters (X), numbers (2), sounds (whistle), or colors. In fact, anything which a person can perceive can be used as a symbol for a concept. A particular concept can have more than one label, and conversely the same label can be attached to several concepts. Marginal cost of the economist and incremental cost of the accountant tend to be associated with a similar concept, while both tend to use the word "capital" to indicate different concepts.

The usefulness of a concept for purposes of research and, for that matter, communication lies, therefore, not in the label which has been assigned to the concept but rather in the meaning associated with it. This point can be appreciated when we consider the problems of communication. For purposes of communication, individuals need to have a means through which they can share concepts. One approach for accomplishing this is through a definition that makes it clear to each how someone else views the pertinent phenomena. Two people can understand what the other means by temperature, if they both define their concept of temperature in terms of readings on a thermometer. They might also attempt to communicate by defining tempera-

---

[6] A. L. Kroeber and Clyde Kluckhohn, *Culture: A Critical Review of Concepts and Definitions*, Harvard University Press, Cambridge, Mass., 1952.

ture in terms of how something feels when they touch it. In the latter case communication may not be as satisfactory as in the former. A bowl of warm water will feel quite different to the person who has been holding a block of ice than to one who has been washing dishes in a sink of hot water.

Fundamental to a definition for purposes of communicating the meaning of a concept is the similarity of human experience. If two individuals' experiences are sufficiently dissimilar, it will be very difficult if not impossible, to develop a satisfactory definition which will allow them to understand each other. For instance, if the concept "temperature" is defined in terms of readings on a thermometer, communication cannot take place if either individual is unfamiliar with a thermometer. The cost of an item defined in Mexican pesos will not be meaningful to a person whose experience is limited to defining cost in terms of dollars.

The following anecdote illustrates the difficulty of communicating a concept between people who have not shared a common experience:

A blind man asked someone to explain the meaning of "white."

"White is a color," he was told, "as, for example, white snow."

"I understand," said the blind man. "It is a cold and damp color."

"No, it doesn't have to be cold and damp. Forget about snow. Paper, for instance, is white."

"So it rustles?" asked the blind man.

"No, indeed, it need not rustle. It is like the fur of an albino rabbit."

"A soft, fluffy color?" the blind man wanted to know.

"It need not be soft either. Porcelain is white, too."

"Perhaps it is a brittle color, then," said the blind man.[7]

A definition, therefore, to be meaningful for purposes of communication, must be prepared within the limits set by the experience of the potential users of the concept, the term "experience" being used rather broadly here and synonymously with background. It would include language, educational, cultural, sociological, psychological, and employment experience. If people's experience tends to differ greatly, it may be quite difficult to

---

[7] Anatol Rapoport, *Operational Philosophy*, Harper and Brothers, New York, 1954, p. 12.

find a satisfactory definition for a concept. An accountant might be hard pressed to find a satisfactory definition for the concept "depreciation" that would be meaningful to a person with no accounting knowledge. This is the familiar problem of defining technical terms for the novice. A similar problem exists in defining colloquial expressions.

For purposes of research, definitions must not only provide for communication but they must also be very precise. Fundamental tools of the researcher are his concepts and he must, therefore, understand them as clearly as possible, not only for communication but also for his own use as well. If he is studying the behavior of customers, he must have clearly in mind what he means by "customer." His understanding of the word "customer" will influence the data he collects and the use he will make of the data. It will influence his ability to communicate with other people. It will certainly affect the relationships he may see between concepts. If a researcher has only a hazy notion of what he means by "customer," the data he collects on customer behavior will tend to be hazy and its value somewhat vague. Any relationships that he may discover and any models he may build will prove to be meaningless and difficult to communicate to others.

OPERATIONAL DEFINITIONS

The problem of effectively defining a concept for purposes of research can be a most complicated business. To appreciate the complexity of the problem, the reader might consider the problem of preparing a statement that would indicate clearly his concept for the very familiar term, "customer." One of the tests of the statement prepared would be whether or not it is sufficiently clear and unambiguous so that several people using the statement to observe the same phenomena would develop the same results. The problem is particularly complicated when dealing with a construct such as personality.

One approach offered for solving the problem of definition is through the preparation of operational definitions which suggest a specific operation for defining a term. Time might then be defined as that which is measured by a clock. Colors could be defined in terms of readings on an instrument which measures their wave lengths. Intelligence would be that which is measured by an IQ test. The operational definition might be thought of as a rule or procedure to be followed in empirically identifying a concept.

Insistence that no term of science can be significant unless it possesses an empirical interpretation is the basic tenet of the operationalist school of thought, which has its origin in the methodological work of the physicist P. W. Bridgman, and which has exerted a great influence also in psychology and the social sciences.

The basic idea of operationalism is "the demand that the concepts or terms used in the description of experience be framed in terms of operations which can be unequivocally performed"; in other words, the requirement that there must exist, for the terms of empirical science, criteria of application couched in terms of observational or experimental procedure.[8]

The following are several illustrations of labels for a concept and accompanying operational definitions:

Label	Operational Definition
Customer	X is a customer of store Y if he states in an interview that he has purchased something from Y during the last twelve months.
Regular customer	X is a regular customer of store Y if he states in an interview that during the last year he averaged one purchase per month from Y and his total purchases during the year from Y were over $150.
Loyal customer	X is a loyal customer of Y if in an interview he states that during the last year 60 percent of the items he purchased in a given class of commodities were from store Y.

[8] Carl G. Hempel, *International Encyclopedia of Unified Science,* Vol. II, No. 7, "Fundamentals of Concept Formation in Empirical Science," The University of Chicago Press, Chicago, copyright 1952, pp. 40–41.

Label	*Operational Definition*
Potential customer	X is a potential customer of Y if in an interview he states that he lives within five miles of Y and has available in the course of a year $500 which he is free to spend on the purchase of the class of commodities sold in store Y.

An operational definition can make possible a very precise meaning to be associated with a particular term. It, of course, does not attempt to include all meanings associated with a term by the language. The meaning which each person associates with a term is a function of his whole experience in life; in a way, no two people have the same meaning associated with a given term. In some cases, people may have only an emotional association with a term. An operational definition seeks to strip any meaning from a term other than that meaning implied by a specific operation. Consequently, certain meanings associated with a term are removed for the specific purposes at hand.

In developing an operational definition for a concept, the procedure should make it possible to achieve a satisfactory degree of invariance, so that several people using the definition to collect data under the same circumstances will tend to make virtually the same observations. A high degree of invariance is also achieved when one person, making several observations under the same circumstances, will secure the same information.

An operational definition for temperature, as indicated above, can be the readings on a thermometer and such a referent can give a high degree of invariance. Several people using a standard Fahrenheit thermometer will tend to give very similar reports when asked to measure outdoor temperature. The underlying assumption, of course, is that the group had a sufficiently similar background so that satisfactory communication can take place when asking them to secure data on the outdoor temperature. The degree of invariance will decline, however, as the calibrations are widened so that the observers will have to estimate between calibrations. If the calibrations are set in even numbers the observers will have to estimate odd numbers and fractions, and consequently their reports will tend to vary. If the definition for "customer" is stated so as to include those people who purchased an average of $50 worth of merchandise a month during the last year, invariance could be a serious problem if the observer (data collector) is allowed to estimate purchases of cash customers who cannot recall accurately how much they spent.

Another aspect of invariance is reducing ambiguity to a minimum. For instance, in defining temperature as readings on a thermometer, there could be problems of ambiguity if the definition did not distinguish between the use of a centigrade versus a Fahrenheit thermometer. Ambiguities in measuring outdoor temperature would be introduced if the definition did not indicate where the temperature was to be taken—in the shade or in the sun, in still air or moving air, for example. There can be ambiguity in measuring depreciation if the definition of depreciation does not make clear what is to be done with purchase discounts, major repairs, and scrap value. Invariance is low not because of a problem in accurately measuring the discount, repair costs, or estimating scrap value but because of the ambiguity in the basis for computing depreciation.

The invariance needed is almost always a relative matter. In the example given above, the cash customers' purchases may involve such small figures that they are not worth taking into consideration. The difference between measuring the temperature in the shade and the sun may be so small that the amounts are insignificant. Each of the following referents for time can have a satisfactory degree of invariance under specific circumstances: light years, decades, years, months, weeks, hours, seconds, or milliseconds. For most purposes a satisfactory referent for human age is years. The number of hours involved would give a degree of invariance higher than necessary. On the other hand, minutes would give a degree of invariance for time in a foot race that would be too low.

ALTERNATIVES TO OPERATIONAL DEFINITIONS

Operational definitions, though of great value from an empirical standpoint, do not necessarily represent the only approach to a complete or satisfactory definition. Furthermore, if the principle of relying exclusively on empirical definitions is strictly adhered to, it may not always be possible to define a concept satisfactorily. For example, a special concept that can be difficult to define operationally and which has proven of immense help in the development of science is the construct. In addition to those concepts dealing with highly tangible phenomena which can be readily perceived through such factors as their color, temperature, weight, and size is the construct which deals with intangible aspects of the environment. An example would be the magnetic field surrounding a magnet. Another example of a construct is personality. We can observe manifestations of individuals' behavior through their physical movements or through what they say. We cannot, however, actually observe personality but only aspects or manifestations. Image of the firm, climate of organization, group atmosphere, and "the invisible hand" are all examples of constructs. Though all of them have the quality of being intangible, they are supported by tangible manifestations. Some argue that constructs are not real but imaginary, while others will say that a construct is just as real as any other concept since all concepts are invented ways for thinking about environment. Whether real or not, constructs prove extremely useful in understanding our environment and are certainly dealt with as though they were real. Possibly the construct gives us a better insight into the basic nature of any concept as simply a creature of the mind. (It may be argued that our invented concepts and constructs are the only reality we know. The value of the concept or construct depends however, not so much on whether it is to be considered real or not but rather whether or not it proves helpful in understanding and dealing with our environment and predicting future events.)

Another objection to operational definitions is their failure to incorporate the purpose of the concept and the context of its use:

I suggest careful attention to the terminology just employed. The term is *operational specification,* not *operational definition,* as is commonly used. I deny the possibility of defining anything by announcing a set of operations; the intent of definition is not contained in operations.[9]

---

[9] Roy G. Francis, *The Rhetoric of Science,* The University of Minnesota Press, Minneapolis, Minn., 1961, p. 10.

DEFINITIONAL MODELS

One rather obvious approach is to define nonoperational concepts in terms of operational ones. The volume of some object can be defined in terms of the operational concepts length, width, and height. Density in turn can be defined in terms of weight and volume. This approach suggests a convenient device for defining nonoperational concepts by using what some refer to as the definitional model. The concept "area" can be defined in terms of length and width, and the model for defining area is $A = L \times W$. A definitional model for volume is $V = L \times W \times H$. Profit can be defined in terms of revenues less cost. The model is $P = R - C$. Average cost can be defined in terms of total cost divided by number of units, and the model is $AC = TC/U$.

The definitional model is not concerned with the behavior of the phenomenon itself (as are behavioral models) but rather with methods for regarding the phenomenon. The model defining volume, $V = L \times W \times H$, is not concerned with the behavior of volume. If we cut the volume of a container in half by inserting a wall, the volume itself has been changed but not the meaning of the term volume. If we heat the contents of the chamber and allow the chamber to expand as the contents become hot, the volume will change but not the meaning of volume. The definitional model will apply under all circumstances to indicate the meaning of volume, but it will not explain the changes in the volume. A behavioral model deals with the phenomenon itself and its behavior. A behavioral model, for example could seek to indicate the relationship between the volume of the container and the temperature of the contents of the container. To study the behavior of the phenomenon depicted by the behavioral model, we would have to study the phenomenon itself through experiments. We can study a definitional model without studying the phenomenon. A behavioral model of the consumer might be one that depicts the relationship between consumer income and the proportion which is spent for food. A behavioral model explaining profit changes might depict the relationship between profit and managerial experience.

A convenient way to distinguish between the definitional

model and the behavioral model is to note that the relationship between the concepts in the definitional model is stated without empirical reference. The current ratio is defined by dividing current liabilities into current assets, and the relationship is stated without studying either assets or liabilities. On the other hand, the form of the relationship between sales and advertising is not known until the phenomenon is studied. The relationship between cost per unit and the number of units of production is not known until the phenomenon is studied. In building a behavioral model we frequently make use of definitional models. In the case just cited, a definitional model might be used to determine the cost per unit, cost per unit equals total cost divided by number of units. Very probably, some would not consider definitional models to be models but rather definitions, and they feel that only behavioral models could be considered truly models. In a behavioral model if we do not have information about the phenomena, we cannot, in effect, build a model but only indicate the concepts involved.

DEFINITIONS WITHIN CONTEXT OF USE

Yet another approach to the definition of concepts and possibly a more typical one is to define them within the context of their use. This involves using both operationally and nonoperationally defined terms. It gives the individual a great deal of freedom in preparing the definition, because it allows him to call on a variety of language and ideas to communicate the meaning which he wishes to associate with a term. He is free to discuss both the denotation and connotation of the term.

This approach to the definition of a term can be quite helpful when dealing with a rather complex concept which has a variety of facets. Constructs, such as organizational climate and corporate image, need considerable discussion to make their meaning clear. If we seek to introduce new constructs for regarding some phenomena, a discussion of the term within the context of its use will make it possible to convey effectively the meaning associated with the term. To define intelligence as that which is measured by the IQ test does very little to communicate to another the meaning associated with the term intelligence.

The following five examples demonstrate how the authors sought to define a concept within the context of its use. They illustrate efforts to convey a somewhat complex meaning associated with a term which would be rather difficult to do either through an operational definition or a definitional model. The examples illustrate various linguistic and literary devices to define the concepts.

SELF-AWARENESS *

A basic requirement for interpersonal competence is self-awareness. This awareness influences the individual's stability and effectiveness because, once it is formed, the self influences what the individual is able to "see" in the environment, how he evaluates it, and how he deals with it. If what he is experiencing "out there" is consonant with his self-concept, then he will tend to "see" it in an undistorted manner. If what he is experiencing is antagonistic to his self, it is a threat. The greater the discrepancy between the self and what it is experiencing, the greater the threat. He may respond to a threat by attempting to integrate it with his self. This means that he must change his self, which, in turn, may mean that he will engage in a long and differentially painful process. Another alternative is to protect or "defend" the self from having to change, by "not seeing," distorting, or rejecting what is "out there." In rejecting what is "out there," the individual may be defending his self, thereby, in fact, also refusing to see "what is inside," that is, those aspects of his self requiring denial of reality.

Thus, to reiterate, competence requires self-awareness. But how does an individual become more aware of his self? One way is to receive feedback (or information) from others as to how they see his self and how he affects them. In this sense, self-awareness requires the help of others.

But, in order to be able to receive the information from others, the individual must be able to accept it. By acceptance, we mean that he must receive the message as it is sent with minimum distortion. The individual can minimize the distortion by not being easily threatened by the message. In order not to be easily threatened, the individual must have a relatively high degree of self-awareness and *self-esteem*. He must value himself enough so that possibly threatening messages are received with minimum distortion.

Before we outline a view of how self-esteem may be developed, it

---

* Chris Argyris, *Integrating the Individual and the Organization,* John Wiley & Sons, Inc. New York, 1964, pp. 24–26.

is important to point out that another way to maximize the learning to be received from others is to minimize the defensiveness of others, because the more defensive they are, the more their messages will tend to be distorted. The defensiveness of others can be a function of their own personality defenses and the impact that others have on them. The former type of defensiveness may be beyond our control, but the second is not.

The operational criterion of self-acceptance is the ability to send and receive information to and from others with minimum distortion. In everyday life, this can be accomplished through increasing self-esteem and the esteem of others. The greater the self-esteem, the less the tendency for distortion that is "internally created." The greater the esteem of others, the less the tendency to create defensive conditions that lead to distortion within others.

Here again the environment plays a crucial role. Society may have norms that tend to prescribe how much self-awareness is permissible. In some societies the child is greatly restricted, by the societal norms, as to what aspects of his self he can explore and modify. In other societies the opposite tends to be true. Societal factors may also influence greatly what the individuals will tend to consider "appropriate" exposure as well as "appropriate" feedback. Thus the nature, scope, and depth of competence that the individual may develop is partially influenced by the environment in which he is embedded.

RESOURCES DEFINED *

Dictionary definitions reflect common usage and are therefore an indication of the meaning generally given to words. It is desirable that scientific usage of common words not depart too far from accepted meanings. Typical dictionary definitions of the word "resources" read as follows:

1. That upon which one relies for aid, support, or supply.
2. Means to attain given ends.
3. The capacity to take advantage of opportunities or to extricate oneself from difficulties.

Evidently resources presuppose a person. They are an expression or reflection of human appraisal. The appraisal finds that something can serve as means to given ends, that one can rely on it for aid, support, or supply. The third definition reveals that resources do not necessarily exist outside the appraiser but can be lodged within him. Evidently there are subjective or internal resources as well as objective or external

---

* Erich W. Zimmermann, *World Resources and Industries*, (New York: Harper and Brothers), 1951, p. 7.

resources. Subjective resources play a dual role: a positive one of taking advantage of opportunity and a negative one of extricating the individual from difficulties or of overcoming obstacles or resistances.

Our conclusion may be clearly drawn. "Resource" *does not refer to a thing or a substance but to a function which a thing or a substance may perform or to an operation in which it may take part,* namely, the function or operation of attaining a given end such as satisfying a want. "Resource" is an abstraction reflecting human appraisal and relating to a function or operation. It is akin to such words as food, property, or capital, but much wider in its sweep than any one of these.

Etymologically the word "resource" is related to source. The prefix *re,* meaning "again," suggests dependability through time, as indicated in the word *relies* used in the first dictionary definition. A person may have various sources of income or support, but a nation has resources. The stress on dependability points toward long-run and social implications, not, however, to the exclusion of other meanings. Here any one of the dictionary definitions listed above could serve satisfactorily.

THE DEFINITION OF ECONOMIC PROFIT *

The economic definition of income as the amount which one can consume during a period and still be as well off at the end of the period as at the beginning [10] is not, I think, appropriate for this problem.

First, the values which must be compared at the beginning and at the end of the period are subjective values. They have meaning to the individual but very little significance for anyone else. For most economic purposes, business profit must be measurable according to market criteria; for tax purposes income should, for obvious reasons, be computed in some uniform fashion. A computation of corporate profits according to an objective set of rules should furnish valuable information to the outside analyst or to the prospective entrant into the industry because the basis for the reported figures can be clearly understood. Subjective estimates have their place in the decision-making

---

* Edgar O. Edwards, "Depreciation Policy Under Changing Price Levels," *The Accounting Review,* Vol. XXIX, No. 2 (April, 1954), pp. 267–280. Reprinted by permission of the American Accounting Association.

[10] J. R. Hicks, *Value and Capital,* Second Edition (Oxford: Clarendon Press, 1946) pp. 172ff. See also Sidney S. Alexander, "Income Measurement in a Dynamic Economy," *Five Monographs on Business Income* (New York: Study Group on Business Income of the American Institute of Accountants, July 1, 1950) in which the author leans heavily on this concept.

process of each firm (though this is less clear in the case of large corporations), but objective tests of profitability will continue to have more value for the outsider so long as the bases for subjective valuations are either not disclosed (if they could be) or are subject to bias in the process.

Second, it is useful to regard economic profit as being related to current production rather than to anticipated production. A comparison of subjective asset values at the beginning and end of a period is essentially a comparison of past revenue-cost expectations with current revenue-cost expectations. Thus, income is derived from expected profits (or net receipts) and represents essentially a smoothing out of a series of future profits. Profit is, therefore, a more fundamental concept than income. Further, the measurement of profit, as contrasted to the measurement of profit expectations, is concerned with past, as opposed to future, events. Hence, profit on a current production basis measures the difference between the identifiable value of current output and the value of identifiable current inputs. On the level of the individual firm or industry, these profit figures are meaningful for evaluating the allocation of resources and the composition of output. The aggregate of these figures would be consistent with the concept of profits toward which national income accountants appear to be working.

The identification of inputs and their values is crucial to this view of profit. Identification must be as exhaustive as possible. All inputs (whether the return each receives is a direct payment or an imputed one) that can be identified and for which values can be discovered must be deducted as a cost of current production.

Following this line of reasoning we shall define profit as a residual. It is that part of revenue which cannot be identified as a cost of any particular factor of production. To determine "economic profit," revenue must be measured in current prices and compared with all identifiable costs measured in current prices as well. The current prices applicable to revenue are those which could be *received* in the market during the period. Thus long-term sales contracts, for example, might result in a deviation of actual revenue from revenue at current prices. The current prices applicable to costs are the current market prices which the firm might *pay* for the goods and services the firm uses during the period. Long-term buying contracts and fixed assets purchased in a prior period may give rise to a discrepancy between actual money costs and costs at current prices.

By current cost we mean the cost of purchasing (if such a market exists) the actual factor services used in current production—not the cost of the most efficient factors that might have been used. Hence, technological change creates a problem only if it destroys markets for now-out-dated factor services. Other sources of cost estimates must be found in that event—presumably opportunity cost.

Economic profit, then, is the difference between current revenues and current costs. It represents the difference between the *economy's* current valuation of the goods and services *rendered* by the firm and its current valuation of the goods and services *used* by the firm. Profits computed in this fashion could be aggregated into meaningful totals for industries and would be consonant with the concept of profits desired for national income purposes.[11]

This concept of profit is basic to the argument to follow. Concepts of taxable profit and of relevant replacement cost will be developed in the course of the discussion. We shall assume that the only possible source of deviation of taxable profit from economic profit is the use of fixed assets by the business firm. Other sources will not be considered explicitly, but the treatment accorded fixed assets can be generalized for other kinds of deviations as well.

COST OR MARKET, WHICHEVER IS LOWER *

The lower of cost or market rule requires that the inventory be priced at cost unless "market" is lower than cost in which case the inventory is to be priced at "market." In retailing, the term "market" as used in this rule refers to the market in which the goods were purchased, not the market in which they are to be sold; in manufacturing, the term refers to cost to reproduce. Thus the rule really means that goods are to be priced at cost or cost to replace, whichever is the lower.

For example, material that cost $1.00 a unit when purchased, which can now be sold for $1.15, and which can be replaced for $0.90, should be priced at $0.90 for inventory purposes under the lower of cost or market rule. The intention behind this pricing method is to protect the concern's normal rate of gross profit in the future. A decline in replacement costs either reflects or forecasts a decline in sales prices. By the time the goods now in stock are sold, reduced sales prices may be in effect. Therefore, to insure that the company will continue to obtain the same rate of gross profit, the inventory must be reduced to its present replacement cost. In so reducing the inventory amount when

---

[11] Solomon Fabricant has indicated some of the elements of business income which must be adjusted if consistency with national income measurements is desired. "Business Costs and Business Income under Changing Price Levels," *Five Monographs on Business Income, op. cit.,* pp. 143–154.

* C. A. Moyer and R. K. Mautz, *Intermediate Accounting, A Functional Approach,* John Wiley & Sons, Inc., 1962, pp. 151–152.

market is below cost, a more "conservative" balance sheet is obtained; there is little question but that the inventory will yield something in excess of the amount shown.

"Market" is further limited to an amount that "should not exceed the net realizable value (i.e., estimated selling price in the ordinary course of business less reasonably predictable costs of completion and disposal)" and "should not be less than net realizable value reduced by an allowance for an approximately normal profit margin." * These restrictions are intended to cover rather unusual circumstances or cases. The first, "not exceed the net realizable value," covers obsolete, damaged, or shopworn material. For example, an item which cost $1.00 when purchased, and which could be replaced for $0.90, may have a realizable value of only $0.70 because it is becoming obsolete. In this case, the item would be priced at $0.70 for inventory purposes.

The second limitation, "not be less than realizable value reduced by an allowance for an approximately normal gross profit margin," is a deterrent to serious understatement of inventory. In effect it establishes a floor or minimum below which the inventory should not be priced regardless of replacement costs. For example, assume that an inventory item which originally cost $1.00 has a replacement cost of only $0.75. Because of firm sales contracts at firm prices this item will be sold at $1.15 per unit, however, and the net realizable value after deducting the normal profit margin will be $0.90 per unit. In this case the item would be priced in the inventory at $0.90 per unit.

For many years, it was contended that the lower of cost or market should be applied to each individual item in the inventory. In many cases an inventory might be composed of hundreds or thousands of items which meant a well nigh impossible task of pricing. Recently, general acceptance has been given to the practice of applying the rule to the inventory total or perhaps to the totals of major sections of the inventory.

To many accountants this appears to reflect a trend away from the cost or market rule and toward the use of cost. From the standpoint of accounting theory there is little to justify the cost or market rule. Although "conservative" from the balance sheet point of view, it is "unconservative" in that it permits the income statement to show a larger net income in future periods than would be the case if the inventory were carried forward at cost. In the opinion of the authors, the rule should be applied only in those rare cases where there is strong evidence to indicate that market declines in inventory prices have

---

* American Institute of Certified Public Accountants, Accounting Research Bulletin No. 43.

occurred which will result in losses being suffered when disposition is made of such inventories. As a rule of thumb blindly applied to all inventories regardless of surrounding circumstances it can hardly be said to be either conservative or reasonable.

In this connection it should be pointed out that, even under a cost basis of inventory pricing, obsolete or damaged merchandise should be reduced to a realizable value for inventory purposes.

DEPRECIATION *

At first, one may wonder why any Depreciation charges have been made for 1961. The buildings and equipment were newly bought at the beginning of the year, and surely they will not have been worn out already. (There will of course be need to spend money on men to maintain the equipment and keep the factories painted. But their wages are already included in Labor Cost or Miscellaneous Expense and are not included in Depreciation.)

Here is where the farseeing wisdom of the accountant comes to the fore. He points out that not a cent may have to be spent upon replacement of equipment for 10 years, at which time suddenly all the machines may have to be bought anew. It would be nonsense, he claims, to charge nothing to depreciation for 9 years and fool yourself into thinking you are making a nice profit and then suddenly in the tenth year to have to charge off all the value of the machines at once and think you have made a great loss in that year.

Actually, he points out, the equipment is being used up all the time. A truer, undistorted picture of net income or profit will be learned if the costs of the equipment are spread more evenly over its lifetime. The value of equipment declines as a result of age and use; it depreciates from its price when new to its final scrap value. In recognition of this, the accountant depreciates the value of fixed capital items by some *gradual* formula. We cannot go into the various methods that have been used. Here are two widely used ones.

The first is called "straight-line depreciation." Suppose that you have a truck whose cost when new is $10,100, and whose economic life is 10 years; after this its physical life may continue but its economic life will be over, because of its unreliability and maintenance costs. Suppose that its scrap value at the end of 10 years is $100. According to the straight-line method you will each year charge off to depreciation one-

---

* From Paul A. Samuelson, *Economics* (New York: McGraw-Hill Book Company, Inc.), copyright 1955, pp. 100–103, used by permission.

tenth of the lifetime decline in its total value, $10,000 (new price minus scrap value). Thus, $1,000 will be charged in depreciation every year.

A second general method called the "service unit method"—or "unit of production method"—can be mentioned only briefly here. According to this we would estimate the number of miles, or loads, or service units that the truck will perform in its life. Thus, if the truck goes a million miles in 10 years and its loss of value during that time is $10,000, then each mile used up represents about 1 cent. This method has the virtue that during the first year of life of the truck, when presumably it will be used proportionately more than toward the end of its life, depreciation charges will be reckoned at perhaps $1,500 (for 150,000 miles) rather than at only $1,000 as in the straight-line method. Another advantage of this second method is that, during periods of depression when trucks are idle a good deal of the time, the calculated depreciation charges are less, and so the businessman may not be prevented from reducing prices by a misleading overestimate of his money costs.

Although depreciation is usually figured by some apparently exact formula, every accountant knows the estimates are really very rough, being subject to large and unpredictable errors, and involving arbitrary corrections and assumptions. He comforts himself with two thoughts: (1) A rough method of depreciation, like an imperfect watch, is often better than none at all. (2) Mistakes in depreciation will ultimately "come out in the wash" anyway.

Let's see why a mistake in depreciation ultimately tends to correct itself. Suppose that the truck lasts 15 years rather than the predicted 10. We have been then overstating our depreciation expenses during the first 10 years. But in the eleventh and later years there will be no depreciation charged on the truck at all, since it has already been written down to its scrap value by the end of the tenth year. Our profits in these later years tend, therefore, to be overstated by about as much as they were understated in the earlier years. After 15 years, everything is pretty much the same after all.

Except for taxes. Different methods of depreciation result in a different apparent distribution of earnings over time, and therefore in a different pattern over time of corporation income taxes. Naturally a businessman prefers a method of depreciation that will make his income average out more steadily over time—so as to keep his effective tax rate as low as possible and permit him to cancel off losses against profits; and he also likes a method that will enable him to put off the evil day of taxes as far as possible.

This explains why so many corporations took advatage of the government's offer to let them amortize (or depreciate) their newly built plants and equipment over 5 years. They were glad to be able, by charging high depreciation expenses, to reduce their stated profits during the defense emergency when their profits were enormous. They much preferred to take advantage of this "accelerated depreciation" plan so as to shift their profits from those years to later years when corporation tax rates were hoped to be lower.

In ordinary times, the Treasury will not let a corporation manipulate its depreciation charges so as to avoid taxes. The company may select any reasonable method; but having once made its choice, it must stick to it. Many people are today worried about the harmful effects of taxation on "venture capital." They argue we shall get more investment in new tools and create more jobs, if the Treasury is more liberal in letting companies depreciate their equipment more rapidly, thereby saving on their taxes. The 1954 tax bill, therefore, lets you take two-thirds depreciation in one-half an asset's useful life.

The problem with the approach just illustrated in defining concepts is the difficulty of using these types of definitions for empirical research. They may not provide a specific procedure that can be used in observing and collecting data. Even the definitional model is not necessarily empirically oriented. We can develop definitional models without necessarily using concepts which have empirical definitions. The problem, therefore, is finding a means for relating various types of definitions.

No matter how simple or how elaborate an investigator's formal definition of his concepts, he must find some way of translating them into observable events if he is to carry out any research. It is not possible to study "national status gain" or "loss" as such, since these constructs have no direct counterparts in observable events. The investigator must devise some operations that will produce data he is satisfied to accept as an indicator of his concept. This stage of project formulation may require considerable ingenuity, especially if the constructs are far removed from everyday events and if little research using these constructs has been carried out.[12]

---

[12] Claire Selltiz and others, *Research Methods in Social Relations*, Holt, Rinehart and Winston, Inc., New York, 1960, p. 42.

As implied earlier, some may feel very strongly about operational definitions and insist that only concepts with operational definitions can be useful in research. Scientific investigation, however, needs greater flexibility than that allowed by the rigorous adherence to operational definitions. Several approaches to definition are needed. Of critical importance to anyone engaged in scientific investigation is keeping in mind the importance of careful definition of his concepts and the kind of definition that he has used. If he has defined his concept contextually he should remember that he has not necessarily provided an operational device for using the concept in empirical research. On the other hand, if he has given a detailed operational definition, he has not necessarily indicated the full meaning and purpose of his definition. When introducing new concepts there is a need for both types of definitions; however, when using well-known and well-developed concepts, the burden may rest with the development of highly operational concepts.

Whatever approach is taken to defining concepts, the scientific investigator needs to pay very close attention to the problem of definition. By doing so he will insure using labels that have meaning attached to them rather than fall into the trap of using meaningless words—jargon, and gobbledegook. He will also be alert to the use proposed for the concept. Last to be re-emphasized are the problems of invariance and ambiguity which should be solved in defining concepts. These problems can be most complex, especially when we are defining a term within the context of its use. The freedom of this approach allows us to fall into all of the pitfalls of language. Language, like music, art, and sculpture, is a means of communication which allows for a wide variety in interpretation. Scientific research is concerned with precision and accuracy in communications as well as its other activities and the problem of effective definition is quite as important as any other task in the research process.

8

Measurement

The principle that the use of a physician's services is a manifestation of the norms or customs of the social group, if accepted, can provide a basic orientation for studying phenomena. It suggests the basis for the development of a theory. Within the principle's framework we can relate several propositions and from them deduce additional propositions. For purposes of illustration let us assume that we have selected the following three statements as being related to each other by this principle:

1. As the demand for a physician's services by the leaders of social group X increases, the demand for his services by the members of group X will increase and in the same proportion.
2. The influence of the leaders of social group X will be in proportion to the degree to which their behavior adheres to the norms of the group.
3. The norms of social group X change in proportion to the group's adoption of new values.

The propositions become the axioms of our theory from which we can deduce additional propositions or theorems. We could, for example, deduce the following:

1. As the values of a group change, the influence of the leadership itself will tend to change either in its influence or in its structure.
2. As the values of the group change, the demand for the physician's services will tend to fluctuate.

Each of these statements in the theory just set forth are verbal models. They indicate in a general way the pattern or the form of the relationship prevailing among the concepts. These models provide possible hypotheses which can be used to study our phenomena. If we wish to do this, however, we would need to gather empirical information on the various concepts and particularly on each concept in relation to the other concepts. In the instance of the first axiom, one would need to have information on what constitutes demand for a physician's services by the members of a social group, what constitutes the change in the demand for his services by the leaders of the group, and what is the nature of the proportional relationship which the axiom indicates prevails between the two concepts. To make possible gathering empirical information about concepts such as these, it becomes necessary to develop a method for measuring the concept—a method for identifying the concept and a method for noting variations in the concept.

The measurement of a concept can be accomplished through a variety of techniques. When dealing with highly operational concepts, the method may not be particularly complex. Total sales per day could be measured through totaling receipts of each day, total personnel may be determined through counting the number of people who received a pay check during the month, and total traffic through an airport might be determined by counting the arrivals and departures.

As a rule, however, the concepts that we wish to measure in business research cannot be approached as easily as in the case of the examples just given. One of the first problems is that, even with rather operational concepts, the behavior of the phenomena is such that it may be difficult to get a measure that is representative. An illustration would be an attempt to measure the proportion of a store's customers that come from a certain section of the community. Since the proportion is not a static figure but a dynamic one that conceptually, at least, could change from hour to hour, some technique must be developed that will provide meaningful information on the concept. A continuous random sampling device might provide information which could indicate the proportion and changes in the proportion. A similar problem is that of identifying defects in the production line. Again the proportion of defects is not necessarily a static figure. One approach would be to maintain a continuous count of all defective items produced. Another approach would be to adopt a sampling device. In either case, we might be able to develop a technique which would indicate the proportion and changes in the proportion through time.

As difficult as the problems might be in attempting to develop a technique for identifying fairly operational concepts, the problem becomes considerably more difficult as we seek to measure more abstract concepts such as constructs. Constructs cannot be measured directly but only identified through various manifestations of the construct. Profit cannot be measured directly. It can be identified only through measuring operational concepts. In identifying the attitude of the employee toward the company, we cannot actually measure the attitude, since it is a function of the various operations and activities in his mind. Instead we seek to identify the employee's attitude through his verbal expressions, his physical behavior, and the verbal expressions of others. On the basis of measuring these phenomena, we then seek to infer what his attitude is. A complicated problem is measuring depreciation of equipment. This is a rather hazy concept at best. Most machinery, unlike the one-horse shay, is not made so that all parts wear out at the same time. What is worse, it is not really possible to measure the degree of depreciation of each part let alone the depreciation of the entire machine. Again there is the problem of finding a measuring method from which we can draw inferences. The degree of depreciation, for example, of an automobile could be inferred from measuring the expenditures for maintenance and repair.

CONCEPT OF MEASUREMENT

In developing a measure for a concept, one is seeking a device that can be used to identify the phenomena referred to in the definition of the concept. The definition precedes the development of a method for measuring the concept. Once we have defined the demand for a physician's services to include, let us say, requests for his medical services, we can then proceed to develop a technique to measure the demand. Since the definition excludes a reference to price or fee charged, we may seek to measure demand by merely counting the number of patients treated per month.

The definition of a concept gives its meaning, but it does not necessarily provide a method for identifying the concept or changes in the concept. Man, in dealing with his environment, devises concepts to provide himself with a method for regarding phenomena. He develops models to depict the behavior of phenomena. But to test his ideas to see if they coincide with reality or can be used to predict, he needs to have a device for crossing the barrier between his symbolic world and the world of phenomena. He needs devices for identifying phenomena that coincide with his concepts. If he invents the concept, liquid assets, he needs to define it and then develop a technique for identifying and noting changes in the behavior of the concept. The technique might allow him to compare liquid assets from month to month in a single firm or to compare liquid assets of several firms.

Previous chapters have discussed the process of building a symbolic world designed to simulate observed phenomena. In the chapter on definition and especially this one, we begin an examination of the problem of comparing the symbolic world with the "real world." Our axioms and theorems dealing with the demand for a physician's services are verbal models designed to simulate in language the world of phenomena, and through measurement the investigator can test the degree to which they accurately depict phenomena. The construction of a model constitutes its specifications; through measurement it is identified.

A highly operational definition may virtually indicate a procedure for measuring a concept. Length may be defined as the reading on a tape measure calibrated in inches and held in a straight line between two points. Circumference could also be defined operationally as the reading on a tape measure, calibrated in inches, placed around a circle. Sales might be defined as the difference in the amount of cash in the cash register at the beginning of the business day and at the close. As mentioned in the previous chapter, highly operational definitions, however, have several limitations. They do not allow for a more abstract definition and hence a broader definition. The more abstract definition of length as being the distance along a straight line between two points allows for several approaches to measurement —length between the earth and a distant planet measured in light years, length of a room measured in feet, and minute lengths in mechanical equipment measured with a vernier caliper. More important, however, the emphasis on highly operational definitions tends to obscure the distinction between the definition and the measure. The definition can indicate the purpose, use, and context of a concept while the measuring device is a technique for identifying and observing changes in the concept in the environment. (Measurement can also be thought of as superimposing a concept on the environment.) The same concept can be measured under varying circumstances through the use of different measuring devices. The same measuring device, on the other hand, might conceivably be used to measure different concepts. A flexible tape could be used to measure length and circumference. The value of distinguishing between the definition and the measure tends to support the viewpoint of those who oppose the idea that all definitions must be operational. We probably could argue that a highly operational definition may come close to providing a measure through by-passing the concept's definition, if it eliminates the purpose and context of the concepts definition.

To return to our example—once we have defined demand for a physician's services, we may then proceed to develop or find some technique which will make it possible to identify the concept, that is, the discovery of some technique whereby we can superimpose the concept demand for a physician's services on the environment. All kinds of activity can be going on in and around a physician's office: people coming and going; people being examined; diseases being treated; telephone calls coming in from patients asking for appointments, advice, and information; bills being mailed; payments being received. In all this activity we need somehow or other to find a technique to identify some of this activity as demand for the physician's services. We need a technique which will allow us to isolate and recognize something as demand for a physician's services.

In addition to identifying demand for a physician's services, we also need to be in a position to identify it in such a fashion that we can evaluate changes in the demand for the physician's services. If we cannot do this, we cannot measure very effectively, because we cannot compare. To do this we need to have a property which varies. The speed of a moving object can vary. Noise can vary in decibels. Weight can vary in pounds. We have a measure if, in combining similar items, we can produce a change. Adding six pounds of water to four pounds of water will produce ten pounds of water, a different quantity. We have produced a change, because we were working with six pounds of pure water and four pounds of pure water. The resulting ten pounds of pure water had the same "water" characteristics as either the six or the four pounds had. The ten pounds was no more or no less "watery" than the first. We did not change "waterness," only weight. The weight we could measure but not the "waterness." By adding heat to water we could change the temperature of the water, a measurable quality, but we still did not change the "waterness" of water. Another example of a property that does not change and hence cannot be measured would be the squareness of a square block. A square may change in volume, weight or density but not in squareness. It is square or not square.

The measurable properties of a body are those which are changed by the combination of similar bodies; the non-measurable properties are those that are not changed. We shall see that this definition is rather too crude, but it will serve for the present.[1]

If some property of demand for a physician's services can be found which varies such as requests for appointments, then a scaling device can be adopted. A tape measure can be scaled in the number of inches, feet, and yards; a thermometer in the number of degrees; the demand for a physician's service, according to the number of requests for services per day, per week, or per month. Through the scaling device, it will then become possible to make comparisons in changes in the property being measured.

---

[1] Norman Campbell, *What is Science*, Dover Publications, New York, 1952, p. 111. (Originally published by Methuen Co., London, England.)

In summary we shall define measurement as a technique which can be used to superimpose a concept on the environment and make possible the identification of changes in the concept. (Even with a concept whose definition is highly operational, we may still have to consider techniques to be used in carrying out the instructions implied in the definition such as adopting a scaling device). The measuring technique will, therefore, attempt to accomplish two things: superimpose the concepts on the environment and make possible identifying various states of the concept. If a concept is not characterized by a property which changes then it cannot be measured.

SOME TYPICAL MEASURING DEVICES

One of the most familiar measuring devices in business administration is the income statement used to measure the performance of the business firm. The measure represents a device based on a rather elaborate set of procedures which are used to measure for some given period, the profits which a firm has produced through its operation. The balance sheet is another. In their textbooks accountants give definitions for the income statement and the balance sheet and a very detailed approach for performing the two measures for these two concepts. Other examples of measures in accounting would include sales, accounts receivable, depreciation, fixed assets, and current assets. In fact, the principle concern of accounting is with measures and measurement.

Other very familiar measures are national indexes of economic activity, such as indexes of consumer prices and the level of production. The Bureau of Labor Statistics has constructed a most complicated method for estimating average prices paid by the consumer and computing an index to represent the average. The Consumer Price Index is then used to compare changes in the average prices paid. The Federal Reserve Board's Index of Industrial Production allows us to compare changes in levels of industrial production.

Students of public opinion devise polls to measure the attitude of the public on elected officials, prominent persons, and significant public issues. A similar type of measure is used by agencies seeking to develop ratings for television programs that can be used to compare the popularity or size of the program's audiences.

In the business firm, efforts are sometimes made to measure performance of individuals in order to compare people or to evaluate individuals for promotions and salary increments. A typical example is the personnel rating form which encompasses an effort to measure several aspects of personnel performance and possibly indicate prospective performance.

Many of the measuring devices used in business administration are drawn from statistical method. Examples include measures of central tendency—means, modes, medians; measures of dispersion—average deviation, standard deviation; measures of correlation; and possibly the best known, sampling.

Always a difficult problem is in the measurement of concepts dealing with human behavior and the attitudes of individuals. An interesting device that has been developed rather recently is the semantic differential.[2] This device is used to measure attitudes of people through asking individuals to choose between a series of paired words. Each of the pairs includes terms with polar meanings and placed with a series of spaces between them. The individual checks the space which will most appropriately express the nearness of one of the two words to his feeling. The closer the check to one word, the closer that term expresses his feeling; and if he checks the space halfway between the two terms, this would indicate a neutral feeling concerning the two expressions.

The rapid growth in the use of mathematical methods of analysis in business research has increased the emphasis on the importance of measurement. The mathematical method of analysis allows us to manipulate empirical findings but these are not a substitute for empirical data. The danger of sophisticated methods of analysis is that the researcher will do more with the data than the data justify. A model built with weak or inappropriate measures will certainly reflect this weakness. Sometimes too much is expected of such well-known measures as the Consumer Price Index.

---

[2] C. E. Osgood, G. J. Suci and P. H. Tannenbaum, *The Measurement of Meaning*, University of Illinois Press, Urbana, Ill., 1957.

DEVELOPING A MEASURE

In seeking to construct a satisfactory measure for a concept or a construct, we need to keep in mind three problems that must be solved: finding a satisfactory scaling device, making certain that we are measuring what we think we are measuring, and insuring that we are doing it accurately—or at least know how accurately we are doing it. If we have decided to measure the demand for a physician's services through counting the number of clients who call upon him each day, we will want to make sure that this technique will measure what we wish to be measuring. We might find that we are really measuring the incidence of disease rather than preference for the physician compared with other physicians. As disease such as flu strikes a community the number of clients will increase, not as a result of an increased preference for the physician's services, but rather as a result of increased incidence of illness. This is the problem of validity. In addition to this problem we will also be curious to know how accurate is our count. We will want to insure that our count does not include people who accompany a patient to the doctor's office. We will want to exclude people who simply returned to pick up a prescription. This is the problem of accuracy. Finally we need a satisfactory scaling device. In this example the basic rules of counting could be used and each client counted as a single unit and all units considered equal and interchangeable. The three tasks or problems in developing our measure are then: the problem of validity, the problem of accuracy, and the problem of a satisfactory scaling device.

If we are using a yardstick made of wood to superimpose the concepts of length on pieces of steel, we will have a satisfactory measure—if the yardstick in truth measures what we seek to measure, if we know the degree of error involved, and if we have a scale that will allow us to make comparisons between different pieces of steel measured. We may find in measuring a given piece of steel several times, using the same yardstick, that the results of our measure tend to vary. The variation may be due to a change in temperature which changes the length of the steel but not the measuring stick. In this case the measure is not satisfactory, because the results of our measure are being affected by a phenomena we have not taken into consideration. We have here a problem of validity. The measure is not valid because we have not properly conceived the problem involved. We have a conceptual error. On the other hand, our measures may vary because we have difficulty in placing the yardstick on the steel the same way each time. The steel or the yardstick are both rough, and hence we have trouble in measuring the same way each time. In this case we have an error in accuracy. The yardstick is an appropriate measure but we have a technical problem in making the measurement. If our yardstick is calibrated only in feet, we will have trouble in comparing measurements of pieces of steel which are considerably less than twelve inches long. If our yardstick is not calibrated, comparison will be quite difficult. This is the problem of calibrating our measure in some way so as to distinguish between different measurements.

We can illustrate these three problems in connection with an aptitude test. Answers on the test may vary each time the same person takes it because of variations in the physical problems under which the test is taken or because of the motivation of the subject when taking the test. In this case we have problems of validity or conceptual problems. In making the measurement we have not taken into account concepts which are affecting the measure. We may also get a problem of validity if the variations are due not to differences in intelligence but due to cultural backgrounds. A problem of accuracy will be involved if a test does not sample enough behavior to adequately determine intelligence. For purposes of comparing the test results of several people, a scaling device will be necessary to distinguish the performance of each on the test; and this can be provided through a numerical score or simply through ranking.

Another example can be drawn from efforts to measure depreciation. If depreciation is measured in terms of both the original and current purchase price, the results could vary considerably. If, due to a change in the value of money, the difference in the results would reflect a conceptual problem in measurement, the differences in measurement would not be a problem of accuracy but a problem of validity. On the other hand, the difference between the two measures may be due to errors in estimating the current value or cost of constructing the equipment. The scale of the measures would be values stated in dollars and assigned by the market or negotiation.

THE ERROR IN MEASUREMENT

The problem of the error in a measure can be dealt with best through determining the pattern or nature of the error. This in itself involves a problem of measurement, because we will be attempting to calculate the variations in the measure and the pattern of the variations. A standard procedure in random sampling is to indicate, in addition to the results of the sample, the error involved. Interpreting the results of a sample which indicates that 60 percent of the population prefer brand x can be appreciably aided if we also know the error involved in the sample. If the chances are 95 out of 100 that the error is no greater than 10 percent the meaning of the measure will be considerably different than if the chances are 65 out of 100 that the error is no greater than 20 percent. Both of these pieces of information will be an improvement over the situation where we have no idea of the error of the measure.

A somewhat different situation develops where we are dealing with a measure which represents a complete count rather than a sample. A census is such a measure. In this case there can be errors introduced by omitting items, double counting, and erroneous counting. If we knew something of the distribution of the error in this type of measure, the meaning of the measure would be considerably improved and, of course, so would its usefulness. An approach to this could be through an attempt to measure the distribution of error. The situation is analogous to the effort to determine the distribution of the error in a situation where we are using a tape measure to measure the width of a room. By taking several measures it is possible to get an estimate of the distribution of the error.[3] The problem, of course, is to get enough information to determine the nature of the error in the measure-

---

[3] This example is given by Irwin D. J. Bross in *Design for Decision*, The Macmillan Co., New York, 1953, pp. 199–202.

ment. This itself is a sampling problem and involves the techniques of statistical estimation.

Another possibility for identifying the error in a measure is to use different techniques to measure the same phenomena. A serious problem in consumers surveys is determining the response error. People frequently give incorrect information either deliberately or through forgetfulness. This response is not revealed by the computation of sampling error. The error can be investigated, however, through securing the desired information in another way. Robert Ferber,[4] in a study of consumer finances, sought to determine consumer-response error through comparing the results of interviews with respondents' finances as recorded by financial institutions. To determine the response error in a survey asking a sample of people where they buy their gasoline, we could add actual observation to the study. It has been suggested that there may be a tendency for people with major oil company credit cards to refuse admitting that they buy nonstandard gasoline because of the status implications. The response error might be checked through actually observing where the people buy gasoline.

Harry Williams and John N. Fry,[5] in estimating the number of tourists who visit Galveston Island, attempted two measures. Since the access to the island was limited to a single bridge and a ferry, a sample of automobiles was taken including estimates of the number of cars representing local traffic and transients crossing the island using the ferry and the bridge. They prepared a second estimate based on use of tourist facilities.

Too often, the problem of error in measurement is given very little consideration. Accountant's income statements and balance sheets do not seek to indicate to the users the nature of the error involved in the figures, but surely no one can contend that there is no error. Bad debt estimates, estimates of depreciation, and

[4] Robert Ferber, "The Collection of Consumer Savings Statistics," (Bureau of Economic and Business Research, University of Illinois). Unpublished manuscript.

[5] Harry Williams and John N. Fry, *Galveston Island Oceanarium, An Economic Appraisal,* Unpublished consulting study, Bureau of Business and Economic Research, University of Houston, Houston, Texas, 1957.

clerical errors in inventory valuation can all add to the error of accounting data. The error in some national statistics can be most frustrating. Changes in the Index of Consumer Prices are difficult to evaluate because of the difficulty of determining the error in the index. The same is true of the Index of Industrial Production, where, however, the error is probably not as great.

Yet, it ought to be clear *a priori* that most economic statistics should not be stated in the manner in which they are commonly reported, pretending an accuracy that may be completely out of reach and for the most part is not demanded. Changes in consumers' total spending power are reported and taken seriously, down to the last billion or less (i.e., *variations* of less than one-half of one percent!), price indices for wholesale and retail prices are shown to second decimals, even though there have been so many computing steps that the rounding-off errors alone may obliterate such a degree of precision. Unemployment figures of several millions are given down to the last 1,000's (i.e., one-hundredth of one percent "accuracy"!), when certainly the 100,000's or in some cases perhaps even the millions are in doubt. All this is stated without any reference whatsoever to the error of observation. It will be seen later that national income and consumers' spending power probably cannot be known now in part without an error of ±10 to ±15 percent. [6]

VALIDITY AND SIGNIFICANCE OF A MEASURE

Determining the validity of a concept is a problem in logical inference. Concepts are abstractions for regarding phenomena, and the measuring device is a technique to superimpose this abstraction on the environment. It does not provide a direct tie from the concept to the environment but only the basis for drawing an inference concerning the logic of the measure in its usefulness to superimpose the concept or identify it. In the simple process of using a tape to measure the length of a desk, we have to make an inference concerning what has been measured. Did the act of measurement measure the concept, or to put the question a little differently, what is the significance of the measurement secured when we placed the tape on the desk and took a reading. We have secured a piece of data on the empirical world,

---

[6] Oskar Morgenstern, *On the Accuracy of Economic Observations*, Princeton University Press, Princeton, N.J., 1963, pp. 8–9.

and we can secure data on the nature of the error—but we are not sure, thereby, of what the data represent. Do they constitute a valid measure of the concept—length, and what is the criteria for determining the validity of a measure? The difficulty of the problem becomes more apparent when we consider the task of measuring a construct such as an organization's aspiration level. Here the problem of determining validity of a measure is difficult indeed.

One solution to the problem is to treat the results of measurement as though they were the concept itself. Then there is no real problem of validity but only the problem of determining the nature of the error and the usefulness of the measurement. Length can thus be operationally defined as the readings on the tape measure. The operational definition and the measuring device are the same. This approach leaves a problem reminiscent of the one faced in considering the significance of a concept. It will be remembered that one value of a concept is to classify, and an operational definition which is a measure can provide a device for doing this. Pieces of wood can be classified according to the reading on the tape measure. A more important value of a concept, however, is its aid in studying relationships, and this suggests a highly empirical approach to evaluating the significance of a measure. If we treat the result of a measure as though it were the concept itself, there is no real problem of validity but only the problem of establishing the significance of what has been measured. Can patterns or relationships be discovered between the results of the measure and the results of some other measure? If they can, and if the form of the relationship is established, we might conclude that the measure has validity. For example, whether or not the concept measured can be used to predict with a satisfactory degree of precision, and whether the error of the prediction can be determined.

If the scores on an aptitude test are used to measure an individual's potential to learn some task, we could consider the score (measure) to be valid if it predicted performance in learning the task or in actually doing it. We might develop a measure to indicate when a machine's useful life is over based on either total repair expenditures or rate of repair expenditures. If in actuality the machine is no longer useful when the standard set of expenditures has been reached, we might conclude that the measure is valid. If in these two cases we could compute the distribution of the error in the prediction, the measure would have solved both the problem of accuracy and validity.

The American Investment Company of St. Louis, Missouri, adopted a system to measure the credit rating of potential borrowers. The system assigns a number of points to a potential customer on the basis of several factors. If the measure successfully predicts good credit risks it could be considered to be valid.

This approach toward validity is referred to by some as pragmatic validity:

In the pragmatic approach to validity, the interest is in the usefulness of the measuring instrument as an indicator or a predictor of some other behavior or characteristic of the individual. For example, tests that require the individual to reproduce a complex design by means of blocks have been shown to be useful in identifying individuals with organic brain disorders. The test-user is not interested in the individual's design-reproducing ability *per se;* he is interested in performance on the test only as an indication of possible brain damage. He does not need to know *why* the test performance is an efficient indicator of the characteristic in which he is interested.[7]

This reliance on prediction as the criteria for the measures' validity can prove useful in applied research where we are building highly empirical models to study the behavior of an operating system or some part of the system. We could measure orders and material consumption and find a relationship so that we might predict with considerable accuracy, material consumption from orders to be processed. A soft drink distributor in West Texas is reputed to have discovered such a close relationship between the weather and soft drink consumption that the weather could be used to predict soft drink consumption. (His system is said to have broken down, however, because of the problem of securing accurate weather forecasts.)

This highly empirical approach, however, has several problems that make it necessary to consider other approaches to evaluating

---

[7] Claire Selltiz, Marie Jahoda, Morton Deutsch, Stuart W. Cook, *Research Methods in Social Relations,* Holt, Rinehart and Winston, Inc., New York, 1960, p. 157.

the validity of a measure. The obvious one is where no relationship is found between the measure and some other concept measured. This raises questions, of course, about the meaningfulness of the measure, since it is being considered as the concept. If we cannot find any relationship between the score on a personnel rating form and some other concepts such as actual performance, then there is some question about what is being measured and the usefulness of the measure. It can provide a device for classification but not for understanding phenomena and predicting behavior. An interesting measure in this regard is the one labeled net profit. Not only are there questions about the nature of the error in the measure but also about what has been measured and what is the relationship of the concept to any other concept. What can we predict, knowing net profit. Has it measured productivity of capital, managerial efficiency, customer demand, careful accounting, or a growing market? The measurement results provide a basis for classification, but the significance is not clear. This would be measurement for the sake of measurement and really not very useful information.

This pragmatic approach can involve some pitfalls. Satisfactory prediction may result from fortuitous circumstances. An aptitude test may prove valid because we are dealing with people of similar cultural and/or educational background. It appears valid because factors which could affect the measurement are unknowingly being held constant. Satisfactory prediction is taking place without any real understanding; and when the measure fails to predict satisfactorily, the problem may be due to the effect of these factors rather than to error in the measurement.

Another weakness in this empirical approach to evaluating the validity of a measure is the failure to integrate the validation with theory and relationships set forth in theory. If we know nothing at all about phenomena, there may at first be no alternative to the empirical determination of validity and relationships. Eventually, however, we will wish to generalize and to develop theory. Measures should be meaningful within theory. This also suggests an approach to the consideration of the validity of theory. In evaluating the validity of a measure we can consider it within the context of the use and purpose of the concept. In evaluating the validity of a measure or in examining the validity of a measure, we will be concerned with studying theory and the conceptual framework within which the concept lies. The more we know about phenomena, therefore, the better will be our position to evaluate the validity of a measure.

Theory can provide a guide to determining validity through suggesting or indicating relationships between or among concepts. If the validity of a measure is brought into question because the errors cannot be determined or because the measure fails to predict, theory can suggest clues for discovering the problem in the measure. Theory in explaining the nature of phenomena provides an orientation for considering what additional concepts might be involved in the measure or what concepts are related to each other. In taking this approach to analyzing the validity of a measure, we will be studying the conceptual scheme involved and the known relationships as well as possible ones in the conceptual scheme. This approach to validation can be a formidable task in that it can include a rather thorough consideration of the entire conceptual scheme involved.

If we have a model drawn from theory indicating that people's banking habits are a function of convenience to their residences and confidence in the facility, measures to identify the model would begin with efforts to measure the three concepts to learn if they are related as theory suggests. By assuming that the error can be determined, the concepts can be studied to consider the manner in which they are related. If they are related as theory suggests, the measures can be considered valid. If, however, they do not demonstrate the relationship suggested, the measures may not be valid or the theory itself may not be appropriate. If there is evidence that the theory in itself can be relied upon, the investigator begins the search to learn why the measures are not valid or simply to develop or use other measures.

In measuring the construct, social status, theory might suggest several concepts which would be manifestations of social status such as education, income, length of residence, profession, and location of residence. The conclusion is that through measuring them we will be superimposing the construct social status. We may add the individual measures together or convert the results into an index. The resulting measure of social status could then be evaluated into terms of other concepts or constructs suggested by theory. If there is a relationship and we can successfully predict it, we may conclude we have a valid measure. If the measure is unsatisfactory because the theory is not substantiated and cannot be used to predict, the measure suggests a re-examination of the construct and the concepts used. It may suggest a complete re-evaluation of the basic conceptual scheme and theory being used to suggest concepts that should be measured. It may be that the idea of social status is not a meaningful way to regard human behavior.

Let us return to the statement that the demand for a physician's services by members of a social group will increase in proportion to the increase in the demand for his services by the leaders of this group. If we cannot successfully superimpose this verbal model on our environment, we cannot establish its correctness as a statement about the environment. We will also not be able to establish it as a valid model. If we are successful in measuring the demand for a physician's services by members of the group and by leaders of the group, in that we are able to determine the error involved, we can then proceed to study the relationship between the two. If we find they are related in the manner of the statement, we may be satisfied that our measures are valid and that the model is valid. If we have trouble measuring the concepts, we will have to examine the techniques of measurement and the validity of the measure. If we cannot determine the error of the measure, we could seek to determine if our measure is valid. We might find that in addition to measuring the demand for a physician's services we may also be measuring the incidence of disease. When incidence of disease goes up, demand by the group and by their leaders also goes up and in the same proportion. We may eventually conclude, in studying the relationship between the physician and the group, that we simply have not developed a satisfactory conceptual scheme for regarding the phenomena.

If the measures are being used to test the relationships suggested by theory and the results do not substantiate the suggested relationship, the problem can be twofold. The measures are not valid or the suggested relationships are not correct. The problem, at this point, is a difficult one indeed. The efforts to consider these two problems should be made in the light of whatever is known. If the relationship seems quite logical in the light of what is known, we may be justified in seeking to develop improved measures. If the relationship is not too well justified by what else is known, it may prove profitable to reconsider the relationship through the addition of concepts or even reconceptualization of the phenomena.

Even where virtually no theory is available, a highly empirical approach is still questionable. Before we can measure we must make some assumptions about the significance of the measure, unless we are measuring for the sake of measurement—which produces information whose value is certainly questionable. In making assumptions about the value of a measure we will be considering the significance, and this significance will be in terms of other measures. Such a procedure will constitute developing assumptions in lieu of theory, but these assumptions will serve the same purpose, although not as satisfactorily. These assumptions, however, will indicate the use of the measure and the context; this will provide the same type of guide that theory would provide in assessing the significance of a measure. Surely this approach would be more valuable and more logical than simply to develop measures and, through uncritical trial and error, attempt to find relationships to establish their significance.

An interesting point to be noted is that, in studying a measure, we might find that it correlates well with a concept which we might not have originally considered relevant. This empirical result could then suggest that the theoretical conceptualization of the phenomena may need to be revised to take into consideration the concept that was not originally included. The fortuitous discovery of empirical relationships or patterns certainly suggests the possibility that, in the process of studying phenomena, we can begin with simple concepts and measures based on highly empirical definitions and from there build up a theory and set of sophisticated constructs rather than the other way around. This suggests that we will not be in danger of beginning with a theory which is a poor conceptualization of phenomena and hence be set on a direction of attempting to develop virtually impossible measures. Something possibly can be said for this highly empirical approach in the early stages of a discipline's development, but even there it becomes difficult to try to understand a phenomena without beginning to develop some ideas concerning the nature of the phenomena and the kinds of relationships which prevail. It would seem that the two approaches should go hand-in-hand: theoretical developments checked against empirical measures, and empirical measures checked against theoretical developments.

The problem of the validity or significance of measures is too often ignored in business administration. As has been mentioned, the validity of the measures of accounting such as the income statement and the balance sheet is open to considerable question. In the income statement, measures are commingled which represent different price levels. The predictive value of the profit figures is difficult to assess. Many ratios are computed in accounting and finance whose significance is difficult to determine in a precise manner. A good example is the ratio indicating the bad debt loss.

The error of casually assuming validity was brought to the author's attention several years ago by a company manufacturing wax-coated milk cartons. The problem originated with housewives complaining that they were finding wax floating in the milk packaged in paper cartons. The solution to the problem, the manufacturer concluded, was to develop new methods to coat the cardboard with wax and develop a test of these various methods. If one were to find a test whose results correlated closely with the amount of wax found floating in the milk, one might conclude that the test was valid. The test, for example, may be nothing more than a device to scrape wax off of the coated cardboard— based on the assumption that the more wax scraped off, the more the process tends to allow wax to fall into the milk after packaging. We might at least have pragmatic validity if the wax that comes off on the device varies in direct proportion to the amount of wax found mixed in the milk poured from the milk carton. In this situation, however, no effort was made to correlate the results of the test with the wax discovered in the milk. The test was assumed to be significant and the entire emphasis was on determination of the error in measuring the amount of wax being scraped off so as to allow comparison between various methods of waxing. If the problem was caused by temperature changes or jarring, then the scratch test was dealing with the wrong concept.

The publication *Operating Results of Department and Specialty Stores* published by the Bureau of Business Research at Harvard University, includes cost data secured from a large number of cooperating stores. The data are reported in percentages of total sales. For each category the report gives a "common" figure and a "median range." The question to be raised is the validity and significance of the measures. In discussing this with the controllers of several department stores, it seems that one of the principal values of the measures is their service as a guide to evaluating their own figures. To what extent are their costs "in line" with those in the survey. The categories themselves are determined principally by convention, as is generally true of accounting categories for collecting information.

In published reports prepared to provide information on business conditions we will frequently find measures such as "number of freight car loadings," "monthly bank debits," "retail sales," "employment," "electric power consumption," plus composit measures designed to serve as business indexes. The significance of such measures is very difficult to evaluate because of the problem in relating these empirically to other measures. Economic theory provides some basis for evaluating them, but it is limited. Employment has some logic, for example, as an indicator. It can be related to income. Statistics such as these, however, are only too frequently published with insufficient regard for their validity or significance.

SCALING A MEASURE

The third problem in developing a measure (though not necessarily the third in importance or sequence of measure development) is the selection of a scale for the measuring device. Through the scaling device it becomes possible to compare the results of measurement. To compare measures which have been made with a yardstick, we may calibrate the instrument in inches or centimeters. In either case we will have the basis for a rule or procedure for assigning numerals to the various readings made with the measure. The yardstick is the measuring device and the calibration is the scale. The final examination in a course is the measuring instrument, and the method for assigning a grade to the examination is the scaling device.

The scaling device allows us to compare the various states of a measurable property. One measurable property of an automobile is the concept economic value which can be measured through the price system, and the scale is the dollar. The price system is the measuring device which seeks to assign to the automobile a numeral which corresponds to the value of the car. In the process of grading a final examination a grade is assigned, either a numeral or a letter, which will presumably correspond to what the student knows. In the use of either numerals or letters we must adopt or decide on the meaning to be associated with the various letters or numerals to be used. If we use the letters E, S, A, U, and F, we could associate with them the meanings excellent, superior, average, unsatisfactory, and failing. This is the scale, and the measure is then the rule or procedure to be followed when grading an examination in the assignment of one of these grades.

If we can rely on the decimal system as the basis for scaling a measure, we would have available what might be considered an ideal counting device. We could use the simple rules of arithmetic for manipulating and analyzing the measures. It also allows for greater flexibility in the use of mathematics. The scale of a ruler has such a base, whether it uses inches or centimeters. If in measuring two pieces of wood the number 24 is assigned to one and to the other the number 12 is assigned, this means that one is twice as long as the other, that two of the short ones will be as long as the other, that four of the short ones will be equal to two of the long ones, and so on. We cannot use such a scale, however, with many measuring devices. For example, in using an examination to measure learning, assigning the letters E, S, A, U, and F cannot be as precise about the difference between the letters. E is greater than S, but it is not very clear how much. Also E is greater than S, and S is greater than A, but we may not be able to say that the difference between E and S is the same as between S and A. Even if we were to assign numerals from 1 to 100 to the performance on the test, we cannot take full advantage of the decimal system. The nature of the measuring device does not allow us to do this, because it is not possible to find the same correspondence between levels of performance and the decimal scales. The nature of the empirical data will not allow this. A score of 100 by one person does not necessarily mean that twice as much was learned as another with a score of 50. Zero does not necessarily mean nothing was learned.

It is sometimes suggested that if we cannot successfully find a relationship between various levels of a measurable property and a scale such as the decimal scale, we cannot effectively measure. This is too limited a concept and, at least in the social sciences, would unduly restrict measurement. Actually, several types of scales are available.

The type of scale achieved when we deputize the numerals to serve as representatives for a state of affairs in nature depends upon the character of the basic empirical operations performed on nature. These operations are limited ordinarily by the peculiarities of the thing being scaled and by our choice of concrete procedures, but, once selected, the procedures determine that there will eventuate one or another of four types of scale: *nominal, ordinal, interval,* or *ratio.* Each of these four classes of scales is best characterized by its range of invariance—by the kinds of transformations that leave the "structure" of the scale undistorted. And the nature of the invariance sets limits to the kinds of statistical manipulations that can legitimately be applied to the scaled data. This question of the applicability of the various statistics is of great practical concern to several of the sciences.[8]

In *Research Methods in the Behavioral Sciences* [9] Clyde H. Coombs discusses six approaches to scaling a technique for measuring which expands somewhat on Stevens' four categories.

The Nominal Scale
The Partially Ordered Scale
The Ordinal Scale
The Ordered Metric Scale
The Interval Scale
The Ratio Scale

---

[8] S. S. Stevens, "Mathematics, Measurement and Psychophysics," *Handbook of Experimental Psychology,* edited by S. S. Stevens, John Wiley and Sons, New York, 1951, p. 23.
[9] Leon Festinger and Daniel Katz, editors, *Research Methods in the Behavioral Sciences,* The Dryden Press, New York, 1953, pp. 473–484.

The nominal scale is measurement at a very primitive level. It is concerned only with classification based on concepts. By using this scale objects are compared only as they do or do not fall in the same category. If we used the nominal scale to classify people as to whether they were members of a group, we would classify them as members or nonmembers but would make no effort to indicate to what extent they were or were not members of the group. People could be compared only in terms of whether they were or were not members of the group. In using this approach to classify sales we would classify them as being certain types of sales, that is, credit versus cash sales. The value of this scaling device is the value of classification. It allows us to classify different groups of objects, and if there are in each group objects that fall in the same class, they will be comparable. The classification of credit sales in Company X will be the same type of sales as the credit sales in Company Y. If we seek to gather together the people in eight companies classified as executives, we will be gathering together comparable objects. In summary, the nominal scale is concerned with the classification of objects into a class but does not indicate degree, and so comparisons can only be made in terms of membership in a class. Because it does not provide for comparison, some do not consider it to be a measure.

The partially ordered scale can be used if we can distinguish in a crude way between members of a class. It is used when we seek to compare two objects—where we can consider one as having more ("greater than") of some characteristic than another, but it is not clear how much more. A has more political influence than B, X is more intelligent than Y, market R has greater growth potential than market T, and so forth. This scale can be used in comparing constructs on the basis of measuring operational concepts which are attributes of the constructs. Where all attributes are greater in one than another, the two can be compared. If market potential is measured in terms of population and income, market R is greater than market T if the population and income are both greater. If population is greater but income is less, the two cannot be compared.

The ordinal scale would improve on the partially ordered scale if constructs can be more effectively compared. In the example of the markets measured in terms of income and population, the ordinal scale could be used if population and income could be combined in some way such as an index. In this case we might use per capita income, and then the market potential of all markets could be compared. The use of this scale still implies that we can compare, but we do not have very much information about the relationships involved. R is greater than T but it is not known how much greater. This is the same limitation as that of the partially ordered scale. A personnel rating form can aid one in ranking people but may not help in deciding how much better one person is than another. In this case the ordinal scale is appropriate.

The ordered metric scale and the interval scale differ significantly from the scales just discussed in that they are used when we have some information on the degree of the relationship—not only is A greater than B but some indication of how great. In an organization for example, the ordered metric scale would be used if we were to say that the executive vice president's authority is greater than that of division heads; and that this authority is greater than that which division heads have over department heads. Putting this differently, A has more authority than B, and B has more authority than C, but the authority which A has over B is greater than the authority which B has over C. The interval scale seeks to refine this through, making it possible to compare this interval between A and B with that between B and C. It would seek to assign a numerical scale to the authority of A and C so that it might say the authority of A is of the order of 100, that of B is 30, and that of C is 10. In this way not only can we indicate that A has more authority than B but also how much more. It also would indicate that two people with authority of the order 100 have comparable authority.

The last scale, the ratio scale, in a sense achieves the optimum in a scaling device. In the interval scale although we have achieved a scale that allows us to select comparable items in a class, there are still some problems in comparisons. The IQ test is scaled using the interval scale which allows us to say that if two people make a score of 100, they are of the same intelligence. It also means that they both have the same degree of intelligence beyond that of someone who scores 50. It does not allow us, however, to say that they are both twice as intelligent as the person who scores 50. Similarly, a temperature of 100 degrees is not twice as hot as a temperature of 50. These types of comparison cannot be made because the origin is not absolute zero but an arbitrary zero. A score of zero on an intelligence test does not necessarily mean zero intelligence. A zero reading on the Fahrenheit or centigrade thermometer does not mean zero temperature but represents an arbitrary zero.

If we can build a scale based on absolute zero, we can use arithmetic operations to make comparisons. (It should be noted that the other scales do not necessarily exclude the use of mathematical operations to analyze the relationships.) The yard stick is based on absolute zero and hence allows arithmetic operations. Twenty-four inches is twice twelve inches, and so forth. Presumably when we have been able to construct a ratio scale we have achieved the ultimate.

The selection of the proper scaling device can help greatly in increasing the usefulness of a measure for purposes of comparing and in reducing the error. The error, for example, can be reduced through the use, where possible, of a more refined scale. This will reduce interpolation. The problem in selecting a scale is to select one that is appropriate to the quality of the measure. If the measure is very crude, the most we may be able to do is to compare members of a class rather loosely, and it would be misleading to use a more refined scale. In comparing authority if the measuring device is crude, the most we can do is indicate who has more authority than whom, and it would be misleading to try to use an ordered metric or an interval scale. The grading of examination papers on the base of 100 is an example of using an interval scale (presumably it is not a ratio scale), but such a scaling device may be misleading in its indications of the quality of the measure. The ordered metric or even the ordinal scale may be more appropriate. A scale which is more refined than the measure may tend to indicate that the measure is as refined as the scale.

9

Data Collection

In a study of business decision making, we could begin by visiting business firms and simply gathering information on the decision-making process which at least superficially seems significant—asking executives what decisions they make and the basis for their action, observing them as they go about making decisions, asking other people in the company about decision-making activity, and reviewing minutes of board meetings—and, as we collect the information, carefully and meticulously recording what is learned. When we have finished this undertaking, we could very precisely report the results of our efforts and comment on the implications of the data collected.

The best that such data collecting might produce, however, is an interesting report but one that may not be very significant even though meticulously done. It may even prove to be irrelevant. Scrupulousness in data collection is no substitute for meaningful data collection. For example, the data may fail to reveal patterns and relationships, prove or disprove hypotheses, support theory, improve problem solving, or provide the basis for prediction. It may fail to do any of these things, because none of them were considered as the basis for the data collection. The basis was in fact nothing more than a simple desire to describe the decision-making process. A study so based tends to have limited value because information is collected without careful consideration being given to what facts to collect and particularly to the reasons for collecting them. The value of any data collected depends upon the preparation and planning that takes place prior to the collection of facts and especially on the nature of the preparation and planning.

How much greater might have been the contribution of such a study if it had been guided by a carefully thought through conceptual scheme and set of hypotheses. The concepts might have focused the study on the decisions to invest in new productive capacity and the hypotheses might have related the decisions to the aspirations of management. Another set of hypotheses would have related the decisions to the concepts that management has of the economics of their industry and firm. Yet a third possibility would have been hypotheses dealing with the firm's standard operating procedures for developing information upon which such decisions are based. Of course, all three sets of hypotheses could have been used. In either case the data collected would be specifically designed to test the propositions. The purpose and use of the data would be considered before collection and the data would be used in making decisions about the understanding of the decision-making process.

The importance of carefully planning the collection of data probably seems most obvious and apparent. Superficially this is true; yet it is one of the aspects of empirical business research which is usually done so poorly. Too frequently, business research begins with the collection of facts without carefully considering which facts are pertinent. The underlying assumptions of such business research would appear to be that if enough facts are gathered on a topic or problem, the facts gathered will themselves reveal enough information to understand the phenomena or solve the problem. If a company is having trouble with excessive labor turnover or absenteeism, the solution under this assumption would be to go out and collect any and all facts that "seem" relevant. Far too often, decisions on what data to collect are based on availability with most of the emphasis in the planning stage on securing accurate and complete information. The value of the data to be collected is assumed—almost just because it is available.

For data collection to be meaningful, there needs to be a theoretical justification for the concepts used. This will insure that data collection is based on concepts which are found or believed to be related and hence the data collected will be more than just information to classify. Data collection is one of many tools in research and is not in itself a complete research process.

The significance of the preparation prior to fact gathering— and particularly the importance of the nature of the preparation—can be simply illustrated if we compare the approach of the high-school student with that of the accountant in gathering information on a business firm to solve some problem. The accountant will have more specific ideas about what information to collect and what information will be worth collecting than will the high-school student. The point can also be made in comparing the accountant with the sociologist. In this case their respective preparations will suggest to each the collection of different sets of data, but both sets of data collected could be equally significant. Both the accountant and the sociologist would be in a somewhat better position than the high school student to gather significant data on the business organization, because both would have a background and a frame of reference which would provide them with a conceptual framework for regarding business organizations.

Conceptual schemes as tools to guide data collection will be limited in providing significant information if such schemes are drawn from a system which seeks only to classify. On the other hand, if the concepts are drawn from a conceptual system based on theory, principles, and hypotheses, they can become powerful tools for the collection of data. If the accountant or the sociologist have available a theory concerning business organizations or some aspect of them, they then have an effective tool for data collection. The theory will suggest concepts to be used in collecting data and will suggest their significance, because it will relate the concepts. If the investigator has drawn from his theory the proposition that the quality of management's pricing decisions will vary in direct proportion to the amount of information management has on the trend of unit costs in production, he could gather data on the information which management has on production costs and on the quality of management's decisions. He can then interpret the data collected in terms of this proposition, or he could seek to test the proposition. In either case he has relevant information.

Recently a study was discussed with the author in which the

investigator proposed to gather data on the cost of making installment loans from a number of agencies making the loans and then to simply compare the costs. Such an approach is crude indeed. It began as though there were virtually no theory available on the phenomena, and the concept "cost" was used simply because it had been found useful in other studies. It was not at all clear what was intended by "compare costs" or what was to be learned other than the costs. It would have been much more meaningful to consider first what significance the concept of cost had in studying installment loans, such as its possible relationship to some other concepts. Size of loan, type of loan, or credit policy, for instance, might well have been considered and hypotheses developed. This approach would have been an improvement. Simple data collection on cost would have been unnecessarily primitive, even if nothing were known about installment loans. The truth of the matter is that something is known about installment loans, and it would not be necessary to begin at such a primitive level. However, even if research must begin at this level, the investigator is just as likely, if not more likely, to discover meaningful patterns if he begins with concepts which have been critically evaluated and, at least, their possible significance suggested. Research might start on the basis of nothing more than some concepts borrowed from economics which suggest a model. We might borrow the idea of incremental or marginal cost and its relationship to revenues and credit policy. Simple data collection is a primitive start and can sometimes be justified —but not as often as practice would seem to indicate.

In summary then, when undertaking data collection, the scientific investigator will want to evaluate critically the concepts to be used to determine or suggest their theoretical significance, that is, to use concepts which on the basis of best judgment are significant because they will provide information on relationships. One will find himself pausing to prepare arguments for the use of concepts and to prepare arguments that will relate the concepts to other concepts. His statements will be based on existing theoretical knowledge or on prepared assumptions and hypotheses about the concepts which will set forth a model of the phenomena.

NATURE OF DATA COLLECTION

Essentially data collection is the process of noting and recording sensory perceptions concerning the environment. The perceptions are made through any of the five senses—smell, sight, touch, taste, and hearing. Typically, in business research most data is collected through sight and hearing. The other three senses generally play a fairly minor role, though in some contexts they can be significant. Smell, touch, and taste are frequently pertinent in examining the quality of products—tasting wine, food products, and toothpaste; smelling perfumes, foods, and drinks; and feeling the texture of cloth and the smoothness of furniture finishes.

Through data collection, the empirical sciences and operational problem solvers gather evidence that can be used to test hypotheses and proposed solutions to operating problems. Data also provide assistance in the development of the theories and solutions to operating problems. Irwin D. J. Bross [1] suggests that man deals with a dichotomy, "the symbolic world" and "the real world," and data provide a sensory basis for both developing the symbolic world and testing it against the real world. The suggestion implies the same idea that has been offered by this book: that man, in attempting to understand his environment and in manipulating it, constructs a symbolic world in his mind to simulate the real world. He may use various tools such as pencils, papers, letters, and numerals from the real world to aid him in conceptualizing his symbolic world but it is basically a creature of his mind. Such tools are necessary, because of the various human limitations such as those of memory as well as the ability to manipulate symbols. The ever-present problem, however, is to bring his symbolic understanding into contact with his environment and the only vehicles he has for doing this is through his sense perceptions. He must collect evidence through his sense perceptions and organize and interpret this evidence in order to have a basis for evaluating his symbolic world.

Data collection has virtually no interest for a nonempirical discipline such as mathematics. Mathematics deals completely

---

[1] Irwin D. J. Bross, *Design for Decision*, The Macmillan Co., New York, 1953.

with a symbolic world. It uses elements of the environment such as pencil and paper, as tools, but it does not collect data on the environment. Admittedly, the environment can stimulate the creativity of mathematics, but it is not a factor in testing the ideas of mathematics.

Data collection is of value, of course, to areas other than the empirical sciences and the applied arts. It is of value to the humanities such as art, literature, and music. Since these forms, particularly art and literature, comment on man and his behavior, data are certainly needed upon which to base the comment. History, frequently considered a humanity rather than a social science, certainly has a strong empirical base for its efforts.

The collection of data may be done directly through the sense perceptions or indirectly through the perceptions of others or of equipment. It may be done directly as we note the customers in a store, the dollars paid for an item, the defective items coming off the assembly line, the speeches of leaders, or the complaints of employees. It might be noted indirectly through instruments such as personnel tests, readings on devices that count people going through a door, or even through the reports of other people who themselves make direct observations.

The basic problem in data collection is evaluating the material gathered. The psychologists have shown that human perception can be notoriously difficult to evaluate. For example, there is a strong tendency for people to observe what they want to see. They are conditioned in their observations by their past experience and education. Emotions can heavily influence observations. A well-prepared conceptual scheme, careful definitions, and sound techniques of measurement are designed to overcome some of these problems. Where none are available, data collection can be difficult indeed. An excellent example of the difficulties in collecting meaningful data are the efforts of a researcher to secure facts to be used in studying people's motivations, potentials, and attitudes. Sometimes the most that is done is to rely on intuition to interpret sense perceptions about an individual. The propagandists have taken advantage of this problem of data interpretation to manipulate data and thus create a desired impression rather than to attempt to indicate properly the state or nature of the world.

The problem of evaluating data becomes more difficult as we rely on indirect methods, for the process of communication compounds the problem of interpreting the data. Using other people to secure information can provide the investigator with the most questionable data, because he will be relying on another's perceptions and evaluations. There may not be a problem of deliberate deception but rather a problem of understanding the people he used so as to appreciate their capability as effective devices to collect data. A great deal of business research has been done through this indirect method of interviewing people, and all of it is subject to this serious problem of the person as the proper instrument.

Another problem is to differentiate data from what in fact is not data. This is part of the problem in relying upon people as instruments through which to gather information. When asked what they saw, heard, or felt, they may report what they think they should have heard, seen, or felt. Even if we are gathering data directly, there can be problems in differentiating between data and something which appears to be data. If we measured the length of several steel rods and computed an average, the average is not data if the term is used to refer to a sensory perception. A summary of several speeches which attempts to develop the consensus of the speeches is not data but is an interpretation based on data. This point may seem to be a rather minor and inconsequential one, yet it is most important to differentiate between data and interpretation, inferences, or manipulation based on data.

The process of scientific investigation has developed a number of approaches which are designed very specifically to deal with the problems of data collection which have been outlined. Three of the methods have already been discussed: careful definitions, methods of measurement, and use of theory as a guide to the data to be collected. In addition are the data-gathering techniques. The numerous books which have been written on the various methods and techniques for collecting data testify to the extensiveness of this type. Each of the social sciences and the various fields of business administration have their unique problems of data collection requiring a considerable degree of specialization in the development and use of techniques for data collection. Because of the extensive work that has been done in the development of methods for data collection, it is not feasible here to review the topic, especially since research methods and techniques are not the topic of this book. It needs to be emphasized, however, that there are many approaches available for collecting information; and the researcher needs to be aware of the many possible techniques available.

One of the principal methods for data collection that has been used in business research is the interview. Conceptually this is a device for stimulating a person through written or oral questions to provide data, for example, on himself, on his environment, his reaction to his environment, his feelings and attitudes. The most familiar method for the interview is probably the closed question where a person is asked a question and given a fixed set of alternatives from which he can select an answer. For example, he may answer "yes," "no," or "no comment." Another familiar approach is the open-end interview question where a person is asked a question and allowed to formulate his answer in his own words.

There are many serious problems in using the interview as a method for the collection of data. There are problems of establishing effective communication with the respondent, interpreting answers which the respondent gives, relying on the respondent as a satisfactory observer not only of his environment but of himself. Naïveté in its use can easily provide data which are virtually meaningless.

A method closely related to the interview is the written examination where the individual is given a series of questions to answer. Yet another approach to stimulate responses are the projective devices such as the ink blot in which the respondent is asked to react to an image.

There are, in addition to the interview and projective devices to evoke a person's written or oral responses, other methods for data collection which are quite effective and deserve consideration, especially in the light of the difficulties in relying on people as devices to provide data. One of these is the experimental approach which for so long has been a basic method of the physical scientist.

The usual approach of the experimentalist is to create a situation where he is able to control variables so that he can study the effect that they have upon each other. He may, for example, seek to hold constant all variables but one and observe changes as he alters this one variable.

Many have felt that the experimental approach does not provide a meaningful source of data collection for the student of business administration because of the difficulty in controlling variables. The number of variables may be so large as to prevent control or the nature of the variables prevents satisfactory control. Frequently cited is the problem of experimenting with people. Marketing has, on occasion, used the experimental method to test floor or shelf displays. The difficulty in evaluating the results is that it is not possible to hold all variables constant that are involved, or even know which are involved. We are not sure of the effect on a person's behavior when a display is altered or if he is reacting at all. Stopping and looking at a display do not necessarily mean that the consumer's attention is focused on the product or brand, but rather he may be reacting only to the novelty of change. In the famous Hawthorne experiments [2] where workers' productivity was being studied, the workers reacted to variables other than the ones which the experimenters were studying. No matter how the variables under study were changed, productivity increased. It turned out that the workers were reacting to the fact that they were participating in an experiment, and hence tried to produce as effectively as possible, notwithstanding the changing conditions.

The proponents of the experimental method argue, however, that the technique can be of considerable use in business research, even in the situations where people are involved. They point out that the data collected from the interview method may be so faulty that the experimental approach is a significant improvement in spite of its weakness. They point out, for example, that even though a housewife may say that she buys her groceries at a given store, there is no evidence that she does. On the other hand, the experimental method provides concrete and reliable evidence of behavior.

---

[2] F. J. Roethlisberger, *Management and Moral*, Harvard University Press, Cambridge, Mass., 1949, pp. 7–20.

Closely related to the developments to increase the emphasis on the experimental methods is simulation. Through simulation it is possible to achieve some of the results of an experiment. An accurate simulation of the behavior of decision makers provides a means to study decision making. It is not the same as an experiment because the decision makers are not themselves involved, but the simulation can be used to test hypotheses.

Yet another approach available to business research is observation. In this situation the investigator seeks to gather data through observing people buying, making speeches, working, and so forth. A possible analogy of observation is the work of the astronomer. He cannot control his variables, but this does not prevent his carrying on scientific research or studying the relationships between his concepts. He must test his hypothesis by specifying his conditions and then examining data collected under those circumstances. He must find a time when nature provided the right "experiment" or wait until nature does. If his hypothesis deals with eclipses, he must gather data on past eclipses if the data were collected using the concepts he is studying. Otherwise he must wait until an eclipse takes place and collect his data at that time. As with the astronomer, an alternative for the social scientist and business researcher to the experiment is actual observation of phenomena or through gathering evidence of events.

Although the social scientist finds himself in somewhat the same situation as the astronomer, in some ways his problem is more complicated because he has difficulty in determining which variables are pertinent. His problem is more complex because either the concepts are more complex or he has not yet developed an effective conceptual scheme for regarding his phenomena. Newton's laws of motion significantly improved the work of the astronomer in providing some useful concepts for studying the universe. When Einstein added the concept of relativity, another significant step forward resulted in physics. Sigmund Freud in his work added some concepts which have proven helpful in studying human behavior. Conceptually related to observation is the collection of data from records, documents, reports, letters, and minutes.

The reader no doubt has some acquaintance with methods

such as the field study, the survey, the questionnaire, the random sample, and the interview. The specific problems of data collection in business research can vary considerably because the fields of study vary so. The accountant will collect different data from that collected by the personnel man and will use different techniques. The marketing man interviewing the potential customer will have problems which differ from those of the financial specialist who is studying the effect of different interest rates on proposed capital investments. As varied as the problems of data collection are, the basic problems are the same. The concepts to be used must be carefully analyzed for their significance and set forth in a conceptual framework that argues and indicates explicitly their significance.

DATA COLLECTION IN REPORTING AND DESCRIPTION

Data collection in reporting provides material to fill in conceptual schemes which guide the process. This will be true if the basis of either is a theoretical or nontheoretical conceptual framework. These data are not being collected to make decisions about the framework, hypotheses, or theory. They are being used only to fill in the framework.

If we are preparing a report on the area of a room using the conceptual scheme that area is equal to the length times the distance, then the data collected will be used only to fill in the scheme. The data will not be used to make decisions about the conceptual scheme or the relationships. Of course, the information on the area may be used for a decision such as whether or not the room will be adequate for some facility, but then we have more than reporting.

Accounting provides a very good example of the role that data collection plays in reporting; it has a very well-developed conceptual scheme, and the business firm collects data to fill in this scheme to prepare reports such as the income statement and balance sheet. The data are not collected as a basis for the evaluation of the conceptual scheme or to test any hypotheses. They are not collected to guide a theoretical decision but to provide a means for viewing the organization through a particular conceptual scheme.

The Department of Commerce uses a conceptual scheme to collect data in reporting on national income and production. In its *reporting* function, the department does not use the data to make decisions about the conceptual scheme or the theoretical basis for the report. (In special studies it uses its data for these purposes.)

Of course, the results of reporting can be used to make operational decisions or to evaluate a conceptual scheme. In this event the role of data is more than just in reporting. Then it is being used in problem solving or inquiry or testing relationships. In pure reporting, however, data are used only to fill in a conceptual scheme.

Although in description we seek to do more than reporting, we are not concerned with decisions about the conceptual scheme or with generalizing about relationships between or among the concepts. By means of a conceptual scheme, in description we attempt to collect data to fill in the scheme and thereby provide an explanation for specific events that have taken place. Cyert and March have suggested nine concepts for regarding the decision-making process in the business firm:

1. Forecast competitors' behavior
2. Forecast demand
3. Estimate costs
4. Specify objectives
5. Evaluate plan
6. Re-examine costs
7. Re-examine demand
8. Re-examine objectives
9. Select alternative [3]

In the preparation of a description of the decision-making process of the business firm, we could, therefore, collect data to fill in this conceptual scheme. Using this framework, Cyert and March prepared a description of standard operation procedures followed by a department store's department in conducting these various steps, and then used the description to build a model to

---

[3] Richard M. Cyert and James G. March, *A Behavioral Theory of the Firm*, Prentice-Hall, Englewood Cliffs, N. J., 1963, pp. 84–86.

simulate the economic decisions of the department. The simulation was, in effect, a description of the department based on this conceptual scheme. The data collected did not, however, provide a basis for generalizing but rather the basis for making the description or filling in the scheme. The simulation itself, however, if a valid one, could be used to produce additional data, to check hypotheses about the decision-making process. This data could possibly be thought of as simulated data or synthetic data because it did not represent actual behavior, and would have to be carefully used as a basis for evaluating hypotheses about actual behavior.

Hoggatt and Balderston filled in a conceptual scheme by collecting data on the West Coast lumber industry and thereby developed a description of the industry.[4] They then built a simulation based on the data collected. By using this simulation they tested several hypotheses. The original data was not used to make decisions about the conceptual scheme but to fill it in to provide a simulation which could be used to test hypotheses dealing with the phenomena.

In summary the problem in either reporting or description is the availability of a conceptual scheme and a method of data collection that will make it possible to fill in a conceptual scheme. If the concepts in the scheme cannot be made operational or if there are constructs for which operational concepts cannot be developed then, of course, reporting and description cannot be conducted. Both of these activities are highly empirical, and their success depends upon the availability of highly empirical concepts.

One of the problems in using some economic concepts in accounting and hence in its reporting function is the difficulty of making them operational. Marginal cost and marginal revenue are typical concepts which are quite basic to price theory but are infrequently used in accounting because of the difficulty of making them operational. The process of determining the marginal cost and the marginal revenue of one more customer in a department store, to use an extreme example, can be most difficult. Or

---

[4] Frederick E. Balderston and Austin C. Hoggatt, *Simulation of Market Processes,* Institute of Business and Economic Research, University of California, Berkeley, Calif., 1962.

being somewhat more practical and suggesting the use of these two concepts to evaluate the addition of a new floor or wing can be almost as difficult.

DATA COLLECTION IN INQUIRY OR QUALITATIVE RESEARCH

The contribution of data collection to increasing knowledge becomes most significant in scientific inquiry or qualitative research. As will be recalled, scientific inquiry is concerned with the development and formulation of concepts, principles, hypotheses, and theories. This activity seeks to structure man's symbolic world. Data can, therefore, provide raw material to stimulate this creative process. Logically, we could use both the results of reporting and description to provide material for inquiry.

The process of inquiry searches through what is known theoretically and empirically to develop additional ideas that can be used in building theory. Where theory is well developed and sophisticated data have been collected, inquiry can be conducted at a very high level. Albert Einstein, in his inquiry which led to the development of the theory of relativity, was working with well-developed theory and data collection based on theory. Keynes too, was working with well-developed theory and data collection based on the theory.

Inquiry, however, can proceed at a very elementary level. In the early development of a discipline, when it has not yet developed any special concepts or hypotheses of significance—not to speak of theories, principles, and laws—investigators will be seeking to familiarize themselves with some of the more superficial and obvious aspects of the phenomena. If we were beginning the study of organizations, we could begin with making what appear to be fairly obvious observations such as size, formal structure, physical activities. In seeking to understand personnel turnover, we could begin by gathering some apparently obvious information on the number of people leaving their jobs, why they say they are leaving, and why their supervisors say they are leaving. These data could then be used to conduct inquiry.

Even in the early or primitive stages of a discipline's scientific investigations, where concepts are borrowed either from another discipline or from everyday conversation, thought must be given to the relevance of the concepts which are to be used. In borrowing concepts we may borrow a model that we feel will be analogous to the new phenomena being studied. In beginning the study of organizations, for example, we might borrow the concept of size from, let us say, physics. Since size has been of value in physics, this suggests that the same concept may be of value in studying organizations. Thus we could begin with the classification of organizations according to size. About the only argument for the use of this concept is that it has proven relevant in another discipline. At a more sophisticated level, we might borrow the idea that size and influence (strength) are related and, accordingly, we might use this idea in collecting information on organization. This approach would entail borrowing an elementary model on the hunch that it might provide a reasonable analog for organization behavior.

Whether data have been collected using concepts which have been carefully selected because of their theoretical significance or for some other reason, they can provide the basis for inquiry. Data revealed in the decennial census of population can suggest valuable ideas. For example, the data can reveal patterns and regularities which form the basis for research. By observing that the birth rates for certain age groups or geographic regions are changing or vary from an average, a pattern to be investigated can be suggested. The investigation may suggest hypotheses to be studied. As a result of working with data, raw material to stimulate insights into new basic principles and concepts for regarding phenomena can also be provided. Two famous examples illustrating the role of data in inquiry are the story of Newton and the falling apple and Roentgen and the X-ray. According to the story, Newton's observations of the falling apple suggested some ideas that led to his work in developing the laws of motion. In the case of Roentgen, he discovered the X-ray through finding some photographic plates near a cathode-ray tube which were fogged. This situation suggested the phenomena which he pursued.

The role of data in stimulating creative thinking is similar to the role of the environment in stimulating the creativity of people other than scientists. Artists, writers, musicians, poets may be stimulated by their observations or, in effect, by data they collect from their environment. It should be emphasized, however, that the role of data to suggest patterns and regularities to be studied increases in importance as one has theory explaining the phenomena. The uninitiated may not note the significance of observed patterns and regularities. Had Roentgen known less physics, he may not have noted the fogged plates' significance. No doubt this is true of other fields. The more a composer knows about music the more meaningfully he can interpret and use suggestions from his environment.

DATA COLLECTION IN TESTING, QUANTITATIVE RESEARCH

Another objective of data collection in basic research is its use to test ideas which have been developed in inquiry. This is the use of data typically associated only with basic research in the physical sciences. In the social sciences and business administration, data collection in basic research tends to be associated more with inquiry, reporting, and description. Testing or quantitative research seeks to secure data to test ideas to determine the extent to which they provide a meaningful explanation of the real world. Inquiry builds a symbolic world to provide man with a basis for understanding phenomena, and testing examines empirically this symbolic world.

The problems of definition and measurement become very critical in this aspect of research for it is here that scientific investigation seeks to bring the symbolic world and the real world into contact. It is important in this type of research to proceed with as carefully considered a conceptual scheme and theory as is available. This type of research brings together man's creative imagination to structure an explanation for phenomena with his ingenuity for collecting data to test his explanation. Data are used to fill in a conceptual scheme and then to test relationships.

The problem in data collection to test ideas is deciding when enough data have been collected to make a decision on the idea being tested. Since scientific investigation can never gather all the data possible to test an idea, it must formulate a criteria for stopping and making a decision. When, for example, have enough data been collected to conclude that under certain conditions a body falling in a vacuum accelerates at the rate of thirty-two feet per second per second.

The answer to this question is implied by the following statement made by Campbell: "Science is the study of those judgements concerning which universal agreement can be obtained." [5] He has in mind not judgments concerning specific historic events but judgments concerning relationships which prevail between specific kinds of events. To use his example, science would be interested in securing universal agreement on a proposition that if a book is pushed off a table it will fall to the floor and not the specific historic event that a particular book was pushed off a particular table and fell to the floor.

Campbell felt this criteria to be a critical point in the process of scientific investigation. He said "When the possibility of applying the strict criteria of universal agreement was realized, then, for the first time in the history of thought, science became truly scientific and separated itself from other studies." [6] In the area of advertising, for example, Campbell's approach would suggest that if we wish to secure universal agreement on the relationship between the events, advertising and consumer behavior, we would have to determine some way to secure the appropriate data to support the judgment that they are related and to secure enough data. This does not mean that we would be interested just in showing that in a particular situation there was a relationship but rather in developing a generalized statement about the relationship between the two types of events. The ideal approach, of course, would be to secure data to indicate not only that advertising and consumer behavior are related but to indicate quite specifically the form of the relationship. If we can discover and depict the form of the relationship and establish its generality then we can approach the possibility of securing universal agreement.

Campbell's point takes us back to our discussion of the scientific approach to the development of knowledge. From empirical observation science seeks to generalize and particularly about

[5] *Op. cit.*, Campbell, p. 27.
[6] *Ibid.*, p. 29.

the form of the relationships involved. The problem therefore in data collection is to secure sufficient data and the appropriate data to provide the basis for securing universal agreement concerning both the existence of relationships and their form. Assuming we are collecting the appropriate data, then we can direct ourselves to the question of securing sufficient data to meet this criteria. (An important point to emphasize is that quantity of data is not alone an adequate criteria since quantity of data is no substitute for the appropriate data.)

The controlled experiment has proven of invaluable assistance in securing information on relationships and particularly on the form of relationships. It provides a means whereby several people can perform the same act and secure the same information. This method can yield very effective information for testing ideas and securing data upon which to base universal agreement. When we cannot use this means for securing information but must rely on other approaches to indicate the existence and form of relationships, securing universal agreement can be most difficult.

It is here of course where the social sciences differ so markedly from the physical sciences. The social sciences have great difficulty in securing information on the form of relationships to justify universal agreement. The social sciences can secure information on specific events in time but difficulty in securing adequate information on the form of the relationships prevailing. We can indicate what happened to sales in a specific situation when advertising was increased, but we have difficulty in providing information about the form of the relationship which prevailed. Changes in sales could have been related to factors in addition to the advertising or completely independent of the advertising. This problem makes it difficult to establish universal agreement on the relationship between advertising and consumer behavior. We begin to make progress when we can at least isolate all factors but the relationship between advertising and consumer behavior. Generally in situations like this we can develop enough information to secure agreement that there is a relationship, but we are far from securing information that will allow us to make the type of statement such as the following about light: when light is reflected from a mirror, the angle of incidence equals the angle of reflection.

In the physical sciences this data collection to study relationships and patterns is usually done through the experiment, and this is probably the best known approach for doing this type of data collecting. There are, of course, other devices such as interview and observation which can also be used in reporting and description.

Since testing and quantitative research are concerned with the examination of relationships, important tools are the techniques of analysis. Two of the basic sources of assistance in this work are mathematics and statistics. Typical examples of analytical tools in statistics are correlation analysis and the analysis of variance. There are also methods for the analysis of nonquantified data which is of special interest to the social scientist, since he frequently must deal with this type of material. Books on research methods and techniques such as Goode and Hatt's *Methods in Social Research*,[7] *Research Methods and Social Relations* [8] (Selltiz and others), and *Research Methods in the Behavioral Sciences* [9] (Festinger and Katz) deal in considerable detail with problems of analysis of both quantified and nonquantified data. Another very excellent book of special interest in business research is Ferber and Verdoorn's *Research Methods in Economics and Business* [10] and Ackoff's *Scientific Method: Optimizing Applied Research Decisions*.[11]

This discussion of the role of data in research has considered its role in the several aspects of basic research: reporting, description, inquiry or qualitative research, and testing or quantitative research. It would be incorrect, however, to draw the implication that each of these aspects of research are necessarily or always performed independently of each other. On the contrary, they

---

[7] William J. Goode and Paul K. Hatt, *Methods in Social Research*, McGraw-Hill Book Co., New York, 1952.

[8] Claire Selltiz, Marie Jahoda, Morton Deutsch and Stuart W. Cook, *Research Methods in Social Relations*, Holt, Rinehart and Winston, New York, 1960.

[9] Leon Festinger and Daniel Katz (ed.) *Research Methods in the Behavioral Sciences*, The Dryden Press, New York, 1953.

[10] Robert Ferber and P. J. Verdoorn, *Research Methods in Economics and Business*, The Macmillan Co., New York, 1962.

[11] Russell L. Ackoff, Shiv K. Gupta and J. Sayer Minas, *Scientific Method: Optimizing Applied Research Decisions*, John Wiley and Sons, New York, 1962.

can and often are closely related. They can support each other
and furthermore may be done at the same time. Reporting, description, and inquiry can all take place in a single study. The
purpose for singling them out is to indicate the various roles that
data collection can play in basic research. If any one of the
processes were to be emphasized to the exclusion of the others,
serious questions would be raised about the value of the research.
This has been emphasized several times in the book when discussing reporting and description.

DATA AND PROBLEM-SOLVING RESEARCH

Data collection has many of the same uses in problem solving as
in basic research. The fundamental difference is the use of data
to aid in making decisions to manipulate or adjust to the environment, rather than attempting to understand it.

A great deal of applied business research is concerned with
securing information on the operating system, the system's environment, and on the goals of people in the systems or in the
environment. Examples would include securing information on
the operation of the warehouse, employee performance, competitors' attitudes, goals of competitors, goals of supervisory personnel. The approach is to gather data to fill in a given conceptual
scheme. The data are not gathered to make decisions about the
conceptual scheme or any relationships which it implies or specifies. The role of data here is, therefore, much the same as it is in
reporting and description in basic research. The difference is the
reports and description are compiled specifically to aid in the
resolution of operational problems.

As in reporting and description, the collection of the data can
proceed most effectively if the investigator understands the phenomena well enough to know which are the relevant concepts to
use. Ideally this means having a sound theoretical understanding
of the phenomena with which he is working. If the problem
concerns a competitor's decision to cut prices, the analyst will be
in a better position to determine what data to collect to solve the
problem resulting from the competitor's action, if he knows some
economic theory which is pertinent to the situation. If the investigator seeks to get information which can be used to affect cus-

tomers' buying habits, his data collecting activity will be greatly helped if he understands something about the nature of human behavior. This information is typically available from a theory on human behavior.

The value of relevant theory to someone collecting data to solve operational problems is that the theory will include concepts whose significance is indicated by the theory itself. A theory on demand may provide information on demand curves and elasticity of demand and indicate the relationship of these concepts to other concepts. Accordingly, this theory will provide the problem solver with a valuable tool to begin his data collection. If for example, he can secure information on demand so as to construct a demand curve and get some idea of the elasticity of demand, he will be able to determine something of the significance of the data collected. This same theory which guides data collection will also guide interpretation. It follows, therefore, if he has no argument to support his data collection, he will also be limited in being able to interpret the data. In this type of research, theory plays this dual role.

The availability of theory to assist him in collecting data to solve problems and make decisions varies considerably from fairly reliable theory to explain the phenomena to an almost total lack of theory. In a case in which theory is weak or virtually unavailable, the problem solver before setting out to collect data should prepare a set of assumptions to argue the significance of the particular concepts to be used in collecting data. Available theory provides the argument. In most cases the data collector will find himself working somewhere between highly reliable theory and no theory at all. Under such circumstances he will be faced with the problem of using both theory and assumptions to buttress his argument for the particular set of facts which he feels should be collected.

Whether there is pertinent theory available or not, it cannot be emphasized too strongly that a basic part of the process of collecting data for problem solving and decision making is to consider carefully the significance of the concepts. As has been mentioned, the question is answered in terms of the relationship or presumed relationship to other concepts. It is not enough to use concepts simply because they have been used before. To do this and nothing more may mean that the investigator will be using a simple classification system whose concepts are not related to each other; or possibly the relationship among the concepts is not known.

It should be acknowledged, of course, that once data collection has begun there may be discoveries that will suggest alternative concepts. It is argued here, however, that the basic approach to collecting data for problem solving and decision making will be as a rule more effective if we begin with an explicit statement about the significance of the concepts to be used. To proceed otherwise is to ignore previous knowledge and to ignore the basic principle that we can only understand and manipulate and/or adjust to our environment as we are able to construct a symbolic world that seeks to provide us with a simulation of our environment.

Even those who proceed to collect data on the assumption that the phenomena itself will reveal the significant concepts and relationships are themselves proceeding with an analog (possibly a vague one) in their minds about the phenomena but are not making it explicit. If this be the case, then the value of explicitly arguing the assumptions will mean clarifying the logic of implicit models which accompany the usual data collection of business research. This argument in effect says that data collection cannot proceed without some ideas about the nature of the phenomena and hence, even where virtually nothing is known, making this understanding explicit rather than implicit will have the value of checking our logic before proceeding to collect the data and reducing vagueness.

The community or economic survey provides a very good illustration of a study designed to collect data to be used in solving problems which make possible adjustment to environmental changes or make changes in the environment. The study may be designed to encourage industry to locate in the community, or to provide information to use in changing the community itself. This type of study also illustrates the use of concepts whose justification is not explicitly stated but is implied. In collecting data on population, a large number of concepts might be used: age, number, education. The theoretical justification for the concepts seems so obvious that it is not seriously considered. The implied justification is that the concepts are relevant, because they are used so often and probably because they are used by the Census in its reports. If the logic of the concepts were to be questioned, the implied logic may seem so obvious to the user of the concepts that he will question the rationality of the individual raising the questions. Yet the user would be hard pressed to give their theoretical significance.

In a community survey designed, let us assume, to attract industry to the community the traditional concepts for regarding population such as those used in the Census might be inappropriate or only a select few may be meaningful. In the first place, the indiscriminate use of concepts which superficially appear to be the significant ones may inundate the potential reader of the survey with far more information than he needs and tends to confuse rather than aid his understanding of the community. This type of indiscriminate use of concepts explains, in part, the familiar phenomena which faces many executives, namely, finding themselves inundated with a great deal of data but very little information. A typical report on population could inundate a person with data but provide him with very little information. Some of the information may be useful but it will probably be difficult to find and then possibly only by accident. Many a community survey filled with detailed data often collects even more dust because the data collected is found irrelevant by the potential user, or its significance is not brought out for him.

A more meaningful approach to gathering population data for a community survey would be to begin with the problem of determining what aspects of the population are meaningful to industrial location. Either on the basis of industrial location theory or on the basis of assumptions, it may be decided that instead of collecting data using the traditional population concepts of the Census, the more meaningful concepts will be those which deal with the customs, traditions, and attitudes of the people in the community, particularly of the potential labor force and of the community leaders. Neil J. Applegate reported in the September 1955 issue of the *Atlanta Economic Review* on the experience of a company which located a factory in a South Carolina community and shortly after operations began found itself faced with serious labor problems. It turned out that the source of the difficulty centered on the failure of the company to gather information on the work habits and traditions of the local labor force and take this into consideration in its operating plans.[12] The technology of the work required a high degree of coordination between working teams, and to accomplish this it was necessary to have the regular attendance at work of every member of each team. It was difficult to replace absentee members of teams and achieve satisfactory production. The work force, although quite willing to work, continued to follow a former practice of failing to show up at work in order to do something else, particularly to work on their farms. This was a local custom and did not seriously affect the program of other companies for whom they had worked. Another company that located in a small community is reported to have had serious labor trouble because it too did not have the correct information on the labor force. Specifically, this company did not have information on the attitudes of the labor force. According to the story, trouble developed between the employees and imported supervisors. The native labor force became irritated with practices followed by the imported supervisors who were simply conducting themselves as they had at previous company plants where they had held supervisory positions. In neither of the two instances cited would the usual population data provide information on significant concepts of industrial location. A theoretical model of life in a small southern community may have suggested the collection of data that would have helped the companies avoid the problems mentioned.

Data collection based on well-developed conceptual schemes can provide material to stimulate the development of alternative courses of action. This is an activity in problem solving which is quite similar to inquiry in basic research. Data collection giving information on the state of the world can provide the problem solver with a basis for suggesting possible solutions to problems. Data collection used to build an empirical model of a company's inventory operation will provide the basis for insights to solve current operating problems in handling inventory. An empirical model of life in a small community, even though just a verbal model, can provide information to suggest to management ap-

---

[12] Neil J. Applegate, "The Impact of New Industry on the Life-ways of Workers in the Industrial Piedmont," *The Atlanta Economic Review,* September, 1955, Vol. V., No. 9.

proaches to recruiting and training personnel for a manufacturing plant to be located there.

Lastly, data collection is also used in problem solving to test the proposed solutions. The use of data in this context is quite similar in many respects to the role of data in basic research to test hypotheses dealing with relationships. To propose a solution to an operational problem, in a sense, is to suggest an hypothesis. For example, a specific course of action might suggest a means to improve employee selection. Data could then be used to test this proposed solution. The data would not only be used to fill in the conceptual scheme but it would also be used to test the relationships implied by the decision. If the proposed decision suggests the use of some test, data can be gathered to examine the usefulness of the test as a device to improve employee selection.

A proposed solution for a problem may be derived from theory or simply from experience. Theory, for example, may suggest that the degree of cooperation between functions of departments depends upon the ease and frequency of communications. We could, therefore, draw an inference and seek to devise a system which will both increase and facilitate communication. The data could then be collected to test the idea. The problem will be to decide when enough data has been collected to justify a decision on the usefulness of the proposed solution. Many of the same techniques can be used to test proposed solutions as are used in basic research.

APPENDIX *

Theories and Models in Evaluation of Business Operations

DATA COLLECTION AND ROUTINE REPORTING IN THE BUSINESS FIRM

The electronic computer has significantly stimulated the automation of data collection and reporting in the business firm. The

---

* An article similar to this appendix was written by the author for publication in the *Business Review* ("Dynamic Evaluation of Business Operations," Summer 1963, University of Houston).

speed of the computer makes possible the collection and reporting of enormous quantities of data. Therefore the concepts that are to guide data collection must be formed with great care. The indiscriminate use of data collection can inundate the management of the firm with data which are not useful in decision making and which will serve to mislead or confuse decision making.

The availability of computers suggests that additional thought be given to reports that reveal trends and patterns rather than the static accounting reports illustrated by the balance sheet and income statement. These accounting reports do not as a rule indicate trends but rather provide information for a single period of time such as a month or year or in the case of the balance sheet for a single point in time. These reports can be thought of as static reports because they do not indicate trends or patterns of change. If static reports are combined, they can, of course, indicate trends. Comparing in a single report the annual balance sheets for a ten-year period will indicate patterns or trends. Accountants are foremost among those who have felt that this type reporting can provide an important supplement to the more orthodox types of reports.* Cost accountants, for example, often prepare reports on cost which are designed to provide information on trends in the costs of production.

In evaluating the operations of the business firm, management, besides the most current information, needs data which indicate trends. In addition to knowing what revenues and costs were for the previous period, management also needs to know the trends of revenues and costs. Are they increasing, decreasing, or remaining the same. Are profits decreasing or increasing as a proportion of total sales and net investment? The typical example of an approach which seeks to provide this type of information is the plotting of sales data on a graph.

The advantages of this type of information are illustrated by a study which was conducted for a large bank. This bank had a

---

* Bernard Whitney and Marion S. Israel in "A Working Model of the Financial Dynamics of a Business Firm," (*Operations Research*, Vol. 6, No. 4, July–August 1958) discuss a proposal to depict patterns in reports on the financial operations of the firm.

study made to analyze and forecast their more important time and demand deposit categories. The study provided the bank with information on the trends which each of these deposit categories had been following over a period of years, and an indication of the probable direction that these categories could be expected to follow in the immediate future. Time deposits of individual customers, for example, were plotted on a monthly basis for a period of ten years, and then the trend forecasted for the next five years.

The bank's study proved so helpful in evaluating the bank's activities to increase deposits that management decided to have a new periodic report prepared which in effect would keep this study up-to-date. Now the bank's management in addition to receiving periodic reports on the current status of their time and demand deposits receives a periodic report which indicates the trend that the deposits are following. The report functions something like a barometer in that it alerts the bank's management to significant shifts in the trends being followed by the various categories included in the report.

Even though the bank's periodic report on deposit trends is an improved device for making information available to management to evaluate bank operations, it is still a limited tool. The report alerts the bank's officials to significant changes in the trends of the various deposit categories included in the report, but it does not provide an explanation for the changes. The report would be considerably improved if it not only indicated the trend of the bank's deposits but also provided information explaining the trends.

The weakness of a report limited to simple trends is illustrated by management's reaction to the study prepared for the bank. As the bank's officials reviewed the study, they noted significant patterns in some of the categories which they could not satisfactorily explain. In some cases, for example, there were changes in the rates of growth and in others there were changes in the direction of growth. These unexplained patterns focused their attention on the need to secure additional information that would assist them in explaining these various developments. After considering the results of the study at some length, the bank's management decided, in addition to their decision to have the study converted into a periodic report, to have a second study made to explain some of the patterns revealed by the first study. (One of the ideas which they sought to analyze was the possible relationship between the growth or decline of selected economic activities in the metropolitan area and the bank's deposits.)

The second study undertaken by the bank could provide the information necessary for converting the periodic report on trends into a report that not only functions as a barometer but also as a diagnostic device. The second study might, for example, reveal that individual demand deposits are dependent on (or are a function of) average family income, proximity of the bank to a working population, convenience of parking, availability of nearby shopping facilities, total population, and a favorable attitude toward the bank's lending policy. As these various factors favor the bank, its individual demand deposits will grow and the bank will tend to draw customers from competing banks. Such information developed by the second study could be incorporated into the periodic report making it possible for the report not only to reveal changes in the patterns of the various deposit categories but also to give some insight into the causes of the changes. It could mean, for example, plotting individual demand deposits on the same chart with data on family income, and working population.

This type of report will provide management with very effective information to evaluate an operation, activity, or task. It will not only provide information on trends but also information to explain the trends. This report can be used for forecasting and for suggesting what variables need to be dealt with in order to alter a trend. Its value in indicating what factors must be dealt with is probably a more valuable aspect of such a report than its value as a forecasting device.

Such reporting will help to insure that the information management gets will be as meaningful as possible. One of the very significant problems of management in evaluating an activity is that there is too much data and there is no criteria available to distinguish between significant information and useless information. Another way of putting this idea is that management receives a great deal of data—some of which is information, and some is noise which interferes with receiving and evaluating information.

This approach, dynamic reporting, could become quite sophisticated and provide a very powerful tool to management. For example, if the bank's second study were especially successful, it might in addition to revealing the factors affecting each deposit category also indicate the extent or nature of their influence. If the study were this successful, a report based on the study would be extremely valuable. It would be possible with this type of information to actually simulate the relationships between deposit categories and the various other factors. It would be possible to predict the behavior of the various deposit categories with considerable accuracy as information on the various independent factors was developed. If bank deposits increase 2 percent for each increase of 10 percent in working force within a certain radius of the bank, information on the working force would be most important. If it were discovered also that the working population in this area were increasing at the rate of 6 percent, it would be possible using these data to forecast growth of bank deposits. It would also be possible to simulate the growth of bank deposits using several possible rates of growth in the working force.

PREPARING A DYNAMIC REPORT

If a firm seeks to prepare reports to indicate trends and patterns to assist management in evaluating the firm's operations it will need to make a study which will do what both the first and second studies of the bank sought to do. If a firm is interested in a report on sales, it will need to secure information on the trend of sales—but much more important, it will need to determine the factors affecting sales. The real value of these reports depends on the success of the firm in developing this second type of information which is essentially the type of information that the bank sought to develop in its second study. The firm's ability to secure this type of information will be considerably strengthened if it has information about the nature of the phenomena it is studying. One of the best sources for this type of information is provided by theory.

The value of theory as a tool in the development of a technique for dynamic reporting is most important, and it is, therefore, necessary that anyone interested in reporting understand theory and the type of information which it can provide.

USE OF THEORY IN DYNAMIC REPORTING

The role of theory in assisting a business firm to secure information to prepare dynamic reports to evaluate some of its operations can be illustrated by the example of the bank in its efforts to discover the factors which determine the behavior of their time and demand deposits. In the case of the demand deposits of individuals, for example, they would like to know specific information about their particular customers—do they tend to bank near their work, their home, or their shopping facilities. In other words, the bank will be primarily concerned with securing information about the state of the world, but they would be in a better position to secure such specific information if someone had developed a theory about banking behavior of individuals. For example, information that people tended to identify with organizations which are sympathetic with their value systems, would suggest to the bank's management that they question their customers to determine just what image people had of their bank.

As important as theory can be, however, it must be supplemented by assumptions which are usually based on experience. Often the most that the theory may be able to provide is a rather general orientation. In studying customer behavior the most that theory from the behavioral sciences might provide is an indication that often customer behavior is controlled by unconscious motives and the practices of their social peers. It may not be able to say very much about customer behavior in a specific situation. If this is the case, and typically it is, then the firm will find itself faced with two alternatives. It may make assumptions about the nature of the phenomena involved or it may itself undertake some basic research to learn for itself what the nature of the phenomena is. If it takes the latter route, this will mean beginning with whatever reliable theory is available, developing hypotheses, and then gathering empirical evidence to test the hypotheses. As a rule, the business firm has neither time and money nor the interest to engage in basic research and hence it must develop the best assumptions it can about the phenomena with which it is working.

In developing a dynamic report for supermarket operations, the most that might be available in the form of theory would be some rather general theory on economic enterprises but nothing specific dealing with supermarkets. This would then make it necessary to supplement the general theory with specific assumptions based on experience and observations.

If the firm wishes to do basic research on supermarket operations, it can take its assumptions and consider them hypotheses to be tested. On the other hand, it can use the assumptions plus whatever theory is available to indicate what data should be collected in order to build a dynamic report to evaluate supermarket operations. Such a report would then provide information not only on supermarket sales but also information on the trend of those factors affecting the sales. From a practical standpoint it might not wish to have a report for each supermarket, but rather current information on fairly large areas where it has supermarkets located. It may, for example, divide a city into areas on which the report would be based.

The value of basing a report on available theory and explicit assumptions is that it will assure a report based on the best thinking available. Where theory is incomplete, inadequate, or inappropriate, assumptions must be made whether they are explicit or implicit. They are at least implicit, because whatever data we decide to collect, we are unconsciously making the assumption that it is relevant. The value of making the assumptions explicit is that it will focus attention on them, and hence tend to emphasize the critical evaluation of the logic of the assumptions.

Bibliography

Ackoff, Russell L., *The Design of Social Research,* University of Chicago Press, Chicago, 1953.

Ackoff, Russell L., with the collaboration of Shiv K. Gupta and J. Sayer Minas, *Scientific Method: Optimizing Applied Research Decisions,* John Wiley and Sons, New York, 1962.

Applegate, Neil J., "The Impact of New Industry on the Life-ways of Workers in the Industrial Piedmont," *The Atlanta Economic Review,* Vol. V, No. 9, September 1955.

Argyris, Chris, *Integrating the Individual and the Organization,* John Wiley and Sons, New York, 1964.

Balderston, Frederick E., and Austin C. Hoggatt, *Simulation of Market Processes,* Institute of Business and Economic Research, University of California, Berkeley, 1962.

Barges, Alexander, *The Effects of Capital Structure on the Cost of Capital,* (The Ford Foundation Doctoral Dissertation Series), Prentice-Hall, Englewood Cliffs, N.J., 1963.

Bass, Frank M., Robert D. Buzzell, Mark R. Green, William Lazer, Edgar A. Pessemier, Donald L. Shawver, Abraham Shuchman, Chris A. Theodore, and George W. Wilson (ed.), *Mathematical Models and Methods in Marketing,* (Irwin Series in Quantitative Analysis for Business), Richard D. Irwin, Homewood, Ill., 1961.

Bergmann, Gustav, *Philosophy of Science,* University of Wisconsin Press, Madison, 1957.

Bierman, Harold, Jr., Laurence E. Fouraker, and Robert K. Jaedicke, *Quantitative Analysis for Business Decisions,* (Irwin Series in Quantitative Analysis for Business), Richard D. Irwin, Homewood, Ill., 1961.

Bonini, Charles P., *Simulation of Information and Decision Systems in the Firm,* (The Ford Foundation Doctoral Dissertation Series), Prentice-Hall, Englewood Cliffs, N.J., 1963.

Bowersox, Donald J., "Food Distribution Center Location: Technique and Procedure," *Bureau of Business and Economic Research,* (Marketing and

Transportation Paper No. 12), Michigan State University, East Lansing, Mich., 1962.

Bross, Irwin D. J., *Design for Decision*, The Macmillan Co., New York, 1953.

Brown, Robert, *Explanation in Social Science*, Aldine Publishing Co., Chicago, 1963.

Brunner, Karl, and Allan H. Meltzer, "Predicting Velocity: Implications for Theory and Policy," *The Journal of Finance*, Vol. XVIII, No. 2, Chicago, May, 1963, pp. 319–354.

Campbell, Norman, *What is Science?*, Dover Publications, New York, 1952.

Chambers, Edward J., and Raymond L. Gold, *A Pilot Study of Successful and Unsuccessful Small Business Enterprises Within Montana*, Bureau of Business and Economic Research, Montana State University, Missoula, Mont., 1963.

Churchman, C. West, Russell L. Ackoff, and E. Leonard Arnoff, *Introduction to Operations Research*, John Wiley and Sons, New York, 1957.

Clough, Donald J., *Concepts in Management Science*, Prentice-Hall, Englewood Cliffs, N.J., 1963.

Cohen, K. J., and E. Rhenman, "The Role of Management Games in Education and Research," *Management Science*, Vol. VII, 1961, pp. 131–166.

Council of Economic Advisors, *Economic Indicators*, Government Printing Office, Washington, D.C.

Cyert, Richard M., and James G. March. *A Behavioral Theory of the Firm* (Prentice-Hall International Series in Management and Behavioral Sciences in Business Series), Prentice-Hall, Englewood Cliffs, N.J., 1963.

Dean, Joel, *Managerial Economics*, Prentice-Hall, Englewood Cliffs, N.J., 1951.

Drucker, Peter F., "Science and the Manager," *Management Science*, Vol. 1, No. 1, October, 1954.

Edwards, Edgar O., "Depreciation Policy Under Changing Price Levels," *The Accounting Review*, Vol. XXIX, No. 2, April, 1954.

Evans, Marshall K., and Lou R. Hague, "Master Plan for Information Systems," *Harvard Business Review*, Vol. 40, No. 1, January–February, 1962, pp. 92–103.

Ferber, Robert, and P. J. Verdoorn, *Research Methods in Economics and Business*, The Macmillan Co., New York, 1962.

Ferber, Robert, "The Collection of Consumer Savings Statistics" (Bureau of Economic and Business Research, University of Illinois), Unpublished manuscript.

Festinger, Leon, and Daniel Katz, editors, *Research Methods in the Behavioral Sciences*, The Dryden Press, New York, 1953.

Forrester, Jay W., *Industrial Dynamics*, Published jointly by The Massachusetts Institute of Technology, Cambridge, Mass. and John Wiley and Sons, New York, 1961.

Francis, Roy G., *The Rhetoric of Science*, The University of Minnesota Press, Minneapolis, Minn., 1961.

Gibson, James L., and W. Warren Haynes, *Accounting in Small Business De-

cisions (Small Business Management Research Reports), University of Kentucky Press, Lexington, Ky., 1963.

Goode, William J., and Paul K. Hatt, *Methods in Social Research* (McGraw-Hill Series in Sociology and Anthropology), McGraw-Hill Book Co., New York, 1952.

Gordon, Robert Aaron, and James Edwin Howell, *Higher Education for Business*, Columbia University Press, New York, 1959.

Gordon, William J. J., *Synectics*, Harper and Brothers, New York, 1961.

Haynes, William Warren, *Managerial Economics, Analysis and Cases*, The Dorsey Press, Homewood, Illinois, 1963.

Hempel, Carl G., *Fundamentals of Concept Formation in Empirical Science* (International Encyclopedia of Unified Science), Vol. II, No. 7, University of Chicago Press, Chicago, 1952.

Johnston, J., *Statistical Cost Analysis* (Economics Handbook Series), McGraw-Hill Book Co., New York, 1960.

Keynes, John Maynard, *The General Theory of Employment Interest and Money*, Harcourt, Brace and Co,. New York, 1935.

Kroeber, A. L., and Clyde Kluckhohn, *Culture: A Critical Review of Concepts and Definitions*, Harvard University Press, Cambridge, Mass., 1952.

Kuehn, Alfred A., and Michael J. Hamburger, "A Heuristic Program for Locating Warehouses," *Management Science*, Vol. IX, July, 1963, pp. 643–667.

Lazarsfeld, Paul F., and Morris Rosenberg, *The Language of Social Research*, The Free Press of Glencoe, New York, 1955.

Leavitt, Harold J., *Management According to Task: Organizational Differentiation, Management International*, January–February, 1962.

Lewis, W. Arthur, *The Theory of Economic Growth*, Richard D. Irwin, Homewood, Ill. 1955.

McDonough, Adrian M., *Information, Economics and Management Systems*, McGraw-Hill Book Co., New York, 1963.

March, James G., and Herbert A. Simon, with the collaboration of Harold Guetzkow, *Organizations*, John Wiley and Sons, New York, 1959.

Markin, Rom J., "The Supermarket: An Analysis of Growth, Development and Change," *Economics and Business Studies Bulletin No. 36*, Bureau of Economic and Business Research, Pullman, Washington, January, 1963.

Mayer, Kurt B., and Sidney Goldstein, *The First Two Years: Problems of Small Firm Growth and Survival*, Small Business Administration, Washington, D.C., 1961.

Morgenstern, Oskar, *On the Accuracy of Economic Observations*, Princeton University Press, Princeton, N.J., 1963.

Moyer, C. A. and R. K. Mautz, *Intermediate Accounting: A Functional Approach*, John Wiley & Sons, 1962.

Nagel, Ernest, *The Structure of Science*, Harcourt, Brace and World, New York, 1961.

Neilson. William A., Thomas A. Knott, and Paul W. Carhart (editors), *Web-*

ster's New International Dictionary of the English Language, Second Edition, G. and C. Merriam Co., Springfield, Mass., 1956.

Newell, A., J. C. Shaw and H. A. Simon, "Report on a General Problem-Solving Program," Reprint of a paper given at International Conference on Information Processing, UNESCO House, Paris, June 13–23, 1959.

Nordin, J. A., "The Spatial Allocation of Selling Expense," Journal of the American Marketing Association, Vol. VIII, No. 3, 1943.

Osgood, C. E., G. J. Suci and P. H. Tannenbaum. The Measurement of Meaning, University of Illinois Press, Urbana, Ill., 1957.

Paterson, Robert W., Evaluation of Economic Forecasting Techniques, to be published in March or April 1965, Center for Research, University Missouri, Columbia, Missouri.

Pierson, Frank C., The Education of American Businessmen, McGraw-Hill Book Co., New York, 1960.

Quinn, James Brian, and Robert M. Cavanaugh, "Fundamental Research Can Be Planned," Harvard Business Review, Vol. 42, No. 1, Boston, January–February, 1964, pp. 111–124.

Rapoport, Anatol, Operational Philosophy, Harper and Brothers, New York, 1954.

Roethlisberger, F. J., Management and Morale, Harvard University Press, Cambridge, Mass., 1949.

Rostow, W. W., The Process of Economic Growth, W. W. Norton and Company, New York, 1952.

Saaty, Thomas L., Mathematical Methods of Operations Research, McGraw-Hill Book Co., New York, 1959.

Samuelson, Paul A., Economics, An Introductory Analysis, McGraw-Hill Book Co., New York, 1955.

Schlatter Charles F., and William J. Schlatter, Cost Accounting, John Wiley and Sons, New York, 1957.

Selltiz, Claire, Marie Jahoda, Morton Deutsch, and Stuart W. Cook, Research Methods in Social Relations, Holt, Rinehart and Winston, 1960.

Spencer, Milton H., and Louis Siegelman, Managerial Economics, (Irwin Series in Economics) Richard D. Irwin, Homewood, Ill., 1959.

Stevens, S. S. (editor) "Mathematics, Measurement and Psychophysics," Handbook of Experimental Psychology, John Wiley and Sons, New York, 1951.

Tonge, Fred M., A Heuristic Program for Assembly Line Balancing, Prentice-Hall, Englewood Cliffs, N.J., 1961.

Toulmin, Stephen, The Philosophy of Science, Hutchinson's University Library, London, 1953.

U.S. Department of Commerce, Bureau of the Census, 1958 Census of Business, Vol. II, Part I, "Retail Trade-Area Statistics," Government Printing Office, Washington, D.C., 1961.

Wallis, W. Allen, "The Business of Schools of Business," Business Horizons, Vol. 2, No. 1, Bureau of Business Research, Indiana University, Bloomington, Ind., pp. 99–103.

Whitney, Bernard and Marion S. Israel, "A Working Model of the Financial Dynamics of a Business Firm," *Operations Research*, Vol. 6, No. 4, July–August, 1958.

Williams, Harry, and John N. Fry, "Galveston Island Oceanarium, An Economic Appraisal," Unpublished consulting study for the Bureau of Business and Economic Research, University of Houston, Houston, Texas, 1957.

Zimmermann, Erich W., *World Resources and Industries,* Harper and Brothers, New York, 1951.

Index